Down to Earth

Praise for *Down to Earth*

"Nil Demircubuk is a very intuitive person. She wrote this book from the depths of her heart. Often, thoughts and emotions disturb us and stand in our way. If you want to be able to manage your life well, read this book and practice what's in it because it will help you to figure out what to do and how to put your emotions and thoughts aside."
—Meir Schneider, PhD, author of *Vision for Life* and *Movement for Self-Healing: An Essential Resource for Anyone Seeking Wellness*

"A groundbreaking and grounded guide to the power of intuition—Nil Demircubuk's *Down to Earth* is the book I didn't know I'd been waiting for. It speaks directly to the part of me that's long craved deeper listening—in myself and in the world around me. What sets this book apart is its bold fusion of science and inner knowing, intellect, and instinct. With warmth, clarity, and zero fluff, Demircubuk demystifies intuition and shows you how to access it with intention and calm."
—Nancy Ancowitz, career strategist and author of *Business Writing: Say More with Less*

"Here is a book that teaches you how to listen to the nascent voice of your intuition, hone it, and apply it to practical life situations. Nil takes the ephemeral topic of intuition, grounds it in scientific research, adds engaging stories, and shares practical exercises to apply this magic to life decisions. Brilliantly written by a maestro of intuition, this book will touch your soul, and show you a path to live with joy, light, and ease. It has already changed the way I use my intuition in my life."
—Pawan Bareja, PhD, mindfulness retreat teacher at Spirit Rock Meditation Center, trauma resolution practitioner, and upcoming author of *Reclaim Your Power: Resolving Trauma and Building Resilience with Mindfulness*

"A masterful and practical book. Nil Demircubuk makes intuition concrete and accessible so that you can make better decisions and access joy and creativity in every area of your life. Intuition is a vital form of insight to complement logic, reason, and expertise. This is a supremely practical, wise, and joyful book that will help people learn to tap into all aspects of their intelligence."
—Sabrina Moyle, co-founder, Hello!Lucky and author of *Go Get 'Em, Tiger!* and *Sloth & Smell the Roses*

"Reading *Down to Earth* felt like returning to who I am. Nil Demircubuk shows how intuition and logic can work hand-in-hand—something I hadn't given myself permission to explore until now. This book is a wonderful guide back to yourself."
—Senia Maymin, PhD, coach to CEOs of global technology businesses and co-author of the business bestseller *Profit from the Positive*

"What if intuition could be learned? Nil Demircubuk teaches us how. Whether trying to choose an outfit, a career, or a mate, our intuition can be our most powerful guide—once we understand what it's truly telling us. Grounded in science and buttressed by experience, *Down to Earth* demonstrates how our gut feelings can be tempered, trained, and tapped."
—Zachary Shore, professor of history and author of *A Sense of the Enemy: The High-Stakes History of Reading Your Rival's Mind* and *Blunder: Why Smart People Make Bad Decisions*

DOWN TO EARTH

DEMYSTIFY INTUITION *to* UPGRADE YOUR LIFE

Nil Demircubuk

LIBRI
LUMINI

Menlo Park, California

Libri Lumini
Menlo Park, CA
Copyright © 2025 by Nil Demircubuk. All rights reserved.

All client stories offered in this book are composites. No story reflects any specific individual, and all circumstances and names have been changed to protect identities.

Library of Congress Control Number: 2025910588
Paperback ISBN: 979-8-9929608-0-8
eBook ISBN: 979-8-9929608-1-5
Book cover and interior design by Christina Thiele
Editorial production by KN Literary Arts

For my two moms, Annem and Mum, and my nieces and nephews Akshar, Ananya, Anastasia, Can, Carla, Ela, Damla, Dario, Defne, Deniz, Finja, Hasini, Himani, Isabel, Lara, Marmaris, Mine, Nil, and Niels, with love.

CONTENTS

INTRODUCTION

Intuition is a sensation or a knowing that we receive in the absence of a prior conscious thought process. It's an ability we all have that allows us to sense things, gain insights, or come to conclusions without using our conscious reasoning. It has frequently been described as "knowing something without knowing how we know it"—a definition I especially love.

For some of us, intuition is lightning-fast, and we don't know where it comes from; for others, it has a palpable inner sensation—like a settling in the gut or an opening of the heart—that gives us a silent signal to go ahead or pull back and stop what we're doing (or merely thinking of doing). After a job interview or exam, the anticipation of good news can make our fingertips tingle, because we know we made it. Our stomachs tighten when the traffic subtly slows to a crawl as we're driving on the highway. As we continue on, our inner knowing surfaces memories of similar incidents without consciously attempting to, and warns us of the possibility of an accident ahead—well before we've consciously registered what's going on.

In this sense, you can view intuition as a search engine—a Google of our conscious and unconscious terrain that helps us tap into experiences, recognize patterns, and make connections between vast amounts of widely dispersed information. Think of it as a quantum computing system that's capable of comparing multiple potential outcomes and weighing them against each other without any need for conscious analysis.

Maybe all this sounds miraculous and almost unbelievable, but it's true. Our intuition is capable of accessing innumerable details we've stored away in our unconscious and subconscious minds and intelligence of our bodies over the many millions of moments that comprise our lives. We might skim over those details in our day-to-day, but our intuition doesn't. Its superpower is literally the capacity to sift through all of them in a nanosecond—discerning the hidden meaning behind everything from a stranger's facial expressions to brilliant ideas that pop up out of the blue and take us on a detour that becomes a brand-new path.

Scientists have been studying intuition for decades, and metaphysicians have been singing its praises for centuries—but its true utility has always been practical. Getting to know your intuition is like opening the door to your own secrets and stepping into your depths. Being in touch with our intuition is the way all of us were intended to live, although in our modern, purely logic-based world, many of us have forgotten.

Think about when you were a child, faced with the wonders of a world you had no preconceived notions about. You had no problem allowing your intuition (and your imagination, which can be intentionally used as a powerful portal to intuition) to lead the way. But over time, like all of us, you lived and learned and began to predominantly use other parts of your intelligence rather than this most primal one. You were probably told to stop dwelling on nonsensical things and to live in the real world, where linear, logical reasoning is everything. Perhaps at some point, you forgot that you ever had access to intuition.

But don't worry. I'm here to remind you that it never actually went away—and that you've probably been using it more often than you realize.

About This Book

Because intuition is our forgotten birthright, I wrote *Down to Earth: Demystify Intuition to Upgrade Your Life* to remind you that it's not out there on a metaphysical cloud or in a faraway realm. Yes, I'd like to think it's a superpower, but it's one that can be easily accessed, right here and now, to help us experience greater ease, joy, and purpose in our daily lives— to bring us down to earth, where we have an opportunity to truly flourish.

Life is filled with countless uncertainties that can end up making us feel mentally taxed and overwhelmed. Intuition is a faithful compass that can help us navigate the rough waters of life by telling us where to turn and also when to slow down or jump in, so as not to miss any of the opportunities life has in store for us.

This book is meant to help you access your intuition— and know that it's there to guide you. It's likely that this isn't the first time you've read about this subject. However, my approach to intuition differs in several important ways. *Down to Earth* removes intuition from the realm of the mystical. I treat it as one of the many abilities we all have—just like our conscious thinking or logic, or our ability to communicate with one another. And I recommend using intuition along-side logic rather than in its place.

Intuition can often feel very intangible, so my focus is

on offering you tangible steps for tapping into yours. While the first half of the book focuses on the fundamentals behind intuition and the truth about how it operates in our daily lives (without us even knowing it), the second half is all about putting what you've learned into practice, through a medley of techniques applied to many areas of your life where you can reap the benefits of using your intuition.

Throughout this book, you'll find plenty of client stories to bring the principles and tools to life. You'll also read about landmark research conducted on the topic of intuition. You'll gain greater confidence in your skills and guidance on how and when to take action on your subtlest of hunches—especially when you're faced with important decisions and turning points. You'll move through a variety of powerful, practical, easy-to-apply exercises that range from meditative and contemplative to simple tools you can use on the spot when you need to. Audio recordings of the guided meditation exercises can be found at nildemircubuk.com.

See this book as half textbook (for an extremely fun and accessible class, not one you'll have to study and get graded on) and half workbook. I recommend dog-earing the pages, writing in the margins, and even getting a journal that you can use to jot down your notes, as well as your responses to the hands-on exercises. The more you engage with the material in this book, the more you'll experience dramatic changes in your well-being and sense of connection to yourself and the world.

Everything in this book is designed to help you apply the information directly to your life. It isn't just theoretical mumbo-jumbo. It's an actionable toolkit that will help you to become more attuned to yourself and the world around you, whenever you want or need.

My hope is that it will be accessible enough for anyone interested in intuition to pick up and use right away, but I decided to write *Down to Earth* when I had clients and others come to me saying, "I know I have an intuition, but it seems to have a mind of its own! It pops up at random moments, or when I really need a wakeup call—but I can't figure out how to access it when I want and need to."

This book will give you what you need to start intentionally using your sixth sense. It's also a powerful tool for anyone who's struggled to connect with this part of themselves, even though something has told them that it's there, waiting to be discovered. People who are already well practiced with intuition will find playful, gratifying new ways of working with it. And, of course, if you're on the fence as to whether intuition is even real (or if it can work for you), I'm here to demystify the topic and explain its usefulness and universal applicability. I'm also here to pique your curiosity and help open your mind, heart, and gut to the possibilities of a life touched by the practical magic of your intuition.

About Me

I've been practicing and studying intuition, and providing intuitive guidance to others, for more than thirty years. During intuitive-guidance consultations, I empower my clients to get in touch with their own intuition. All my students say that the progress they make in just a few lessons is mind-blowing. They start including their intuition in their daily lives and gain many powerful insights from this practice. They get to know themselves better, build stronger relationships with others, make more sound decisions, and experience a greater degree of fulfillment than they ever knew was possible.

Most of my intuitive-guidance clients and students come to me with some preexisting familiarity with this often-neglected ability. Some of them describe their intuition as a sense of comfort in their body when things feel just right, and an uncomfortable tension when something feels off. Many share anecdotes about such sensations upon meeting a significant person in their life for the first time. "Something inside me had the 'spidey sense' that we'd be instant friends!" "From the first two minutes of our conversation, I just knew this was going to be the person I'd fall in love with." Or, more upsetting but often as common, "Some part of me had a bad feeling about that person right from the start, even though I couldn't put my finger on it. Why didn't I pay closer attention?" In these cases, they knew without knowing how they knew, and events ultimately unfolded to prove their nascent hunches right.

I don't rely on what some might consider esoteric or metaphysical tools to lead my clients and students to the answers they're looking for. Both the techniques and applications stay in the practical realm. I use intuition multiple times a day for making decisions, coming up with ideas, figuring out puzzling situations in my interactions and relationships with others, and having fun. I was born this way, just like you. Of course, as I grew up, the demands of structured education, work, and other rules and regulations got in the way of accessing intuition, as inevitably happens. Thankfully, intuition came back to my life full force in my early twenties, and I have been using it ever since.

Intuition was a constant companion for me when I was a very young child, growing up in my home country of Turkey. I used to get hunches about what to do in potentially dangerous situations, which saved me from getting in big trouble many times. Even playing was an intuitive practice for me. I didn't need toys to have fun. I just followed my intuition to make up games and entertain myself. I could play with a single handkerchief for hours, turning it into a doll, a tablecloth for a tea party, a hat, or a magical superhero cape.

As I grew up, the analytical side of my abilities started to reveal themselves. I was a quick learner and picked up how to read and write while watching my older brother study. I was good at mathematics and loved numbers. In Turkey, that meant my path through college was preordained. I was destined to become an engineer. I dutifully followed this path without questioning it. As I became more and more analytical, my intuition got quieter and quieter.

Shortly after graduating from college, a multi-vehicle car crash that resulted in a severe head injury gave me the jolt that woke me up and reminded me of my intuition. I was half-asleep most of the day for about a week after the concussion. I dozed off and woke up with big ideas and images floating around in my mind. About a year after the accident, I started to have episodes of benign tremors that presented like absence seizures (a form of epilepsy that can cause seizures, abnormal brain activity, and a change in awareness); they grew in intensity and frequency over time. Within a few months, I was having multiple episodes a day and going from doctor to doctor in search of answers—and with luck, a cure.

These episodes were difficult to go through, but strangely, I felt an enormous sense of peace right after each one, which made the ordeal almost seem worth it. Whatever was happening inside my brain, it had the effect of putting my mind and whole being into a very still and calm state. During one of these moments of calm after the internal storm, I started to notice that my intuition was very loud. It felt like I was reuniting with a dear old friend.

My intuition came through in a variety of ways. For example, I had a strong feeling about something troubling a faculty member I was going to work with on a research project. The topic was exciting and ideal for me, but some part of me kept saying to find someone else. I decided to listen to this nudge. A couple of months later, that faculty member had to leave due to personal reasons—and the project was canceled.

Another instance occurred one evening when I was celebrating a friend's birthday. One of my friends didn't seem well, although he wasn't in visible pain nor was he complaining. He finally admitted that his stomach was burning slightly, which he chalked up to indigestion. I felt that it was more serious and insisted on taking him to the ER. He started to feel sick on our way there. He had to stay at the hospital overnight, as it turned out he was having a severe allergic reaction to something he'd eaten at the party.

This was around my second year in a PhD program in economics at Clemson University in South Carolina. My roommates and close friends noticed that I seemed to be getting pretty good at offering clear insights. They called me whenever they needed guidance on projects, potential romantic relationships, or what to say or do in complicated interactions and conflicts with others.

As I became more comfortable with this familiar, old connection with my inner wisdom, I also became curious about it. I sought out and studied with wonderful teachers over the next decade. This overlapped with a period of learning and practicing various energy-work methods, such as bioenergy, polarity therapy, Reiki, and specific types of Qigong. I believed that such work could support and facilitate the healing process in a person's body, mind, and spirit when used together with medical treatments. I didn't see it as giving or transferring something to my clients that they lacked; rather, it was working to fully restore the wholeness that already existed within. I considered this healing facilitation work I was starting to do with clients as a complement to their medical care, never a substitute. I always encouraged my clients to see medical doctors if they had given up on the medical world too quickly and wanted to rely solely on alternative therapies. In much the same way, I see logic and intuition as being complementary skills we should always keep in our back pocket. I kept reminding my clients that we were trying to boost their body's ability to heal with energy work as an addition to and not instead of them getting expert medical care.

I followed my intuition during these healing facilitation sessions. I started to sense things about my clients' lives or states of mind and emotions. When I shared these intuitive messages with my clients, they always appreciated it and could link them to some current reality or memory. Each message also made sense to them, as it somehow related to what they were feeling in their bodies.

During a Reiki session with a client who was in her sixties, I sensed a deep sadness, grief, and fear within her that was rooted in the past. I had the hunch that it was connected to something from her childhood that had been buried—although I had no idea why I thought this, as she hadn't explicitly mentioned anything to me. In fact, abdominal pain was the specific reason this client had come to me. As always, I made sure that she was checked by a medical doctor first before we worked together. Her pain was severe, but the doctors had not found anything wrong with her physically and chalked up her condition as most likely psychosomatic. After her Reiki session, I had a strong sense that I needed to share what I had sensed. As I told her what I'd experienced, she began to cry. She verified that I had indeed somehow connected to a deep sorrow from her past; she had to leave her home, alongside the thousands of people who'd been exiled in her home country. I offered her a safe, compassionate space to process some of these intense emotions. I told her to consider talking to a therapist. She felt much better after that session, and we both knew that her healing had begun through the release of some of those pent-up emotions.

After this experience, I started to seek out teachers who could help me understand the intuitive process more clearly. My intuition guided me in this area of my life as well. While I was reading a book by an experienced teacher, I had a very clear knowing that I needed to study with her. I looked her up, found her website, and there it was: an all-day workshop scheduled in the city where I lived. I signed up and went to the workshop, where I found out about her training program.

I attended the first training I could book. Once that training was complete, I signed up for the next level and went through the apprenticeship program the following year. I approached learning about intuition with the same determination that helped me obtain a PhD despite significant health challenges. I took it on as a research topic, as well as a lifestyle. I got better and faster at accessing my intuition and running it through the filter of my intellect and logic.

As I gained confidence through these studies, I started my own practice of offering intuitive-guidance readings. I showed clients quick and playful ways of accessing their intuition to receive immediate guidance so they wouldn't develop a dependency on anyone else to do this for them. By word of mouth, my client base grew quickly; pretty soon, I was having a hard time balancing my corporate career and my more under-the-radar energy and intuition work, which felt much more meaningful to me.

By this time, I was a senior director at a financial technology company. Part of me felt as if I were torn in two, living a double life. I was a fast-paced corporate manager using her analytical skills by day, and an energy-work practitioner and intuitive guide by night and on weekends. In reality, there were overlaps between these seemingly separate worlds. I was frequently tapping into my intuition at work, especially in interactions with colleagues. I liked being able to sense when my team members were doing well and when they were not feeling at their best. This allowed me to check on them and figure out how we could improve things together before the situation snowballed into a crisis. And at home, in our little guest room turned energy-work and intuitive-reading space, I was using my analytical skills to make the connections between what my intuition might be saying and how my clients were feeling, while also doing my due diligence to ensure they were seeking expert medical advice.

Many years of providing intuitive guidance eventually led me to begin facilitating the process of accessing intuition in a more structured way. One of my clients requested this, and we began our lessons experimentally at first, eager to see where they'd take us both. As she requested more information, I expanded my intuition curriculum. Once the word was out, more people signed up for my intuition facilitation sessions. Over time, the teaching material I prepared for these sessions started to pile up, eventually giving birth to this book you are now reading.

My background in teaching undergraduate and graduate-level courses during my PhD program helped me immensely in learning to develop a curriculum on a subject as deep and elusive as intuition. After my corporate career, I also worked at nonprofit organizations, where I created and led human-rights awareness programs. I taught classes on these topics, as well as on self-confidence and compassion, all of which infuse my work with intuition to this day. Teaching as a vehicle for empowering people is truly my passion.

My experience with a diverse roster of clients has persuaded me that intuition is something every single person alive can learn to consciously access and tap into, not just for their benefit but also for the benefit of the people they care about and upon whom they have ripple effects. It may feel a little tricky at first, especially for people who have lost touch with this intrinsic gift, but it's a lot like learning a language.

The more you practice, the more adept you will become. All it takes is the patience and willingness to communicate with a part of you that has always been there, while offering it the space to pop up and respond.

The knowledge, tools, and exercises in this book are meant to be fun and to give you a crash course in personal transformation and empowerment. I encourage you to approach all of it with an open mind and try your hand at the exercises. I also encourage you to be creative and consider coming up with your own methods of accessing your intuition. Simply let your intuition guide the way and have fun while you're at it.

Thank you for taking the first step toward living a truly enriching life informed and enchanted by the power of your intuition. This book is my natural next step in sharing my knowledge and experience with intuition with as many people as possible. I hope it brings joy, light, and ease to your life.

CHAPTER 1

Listen to You—Laying the Foundation for Intuition

I know something about you that you may not be aware of yet. Science backs me up on this too. You have a wise sage living within you. This inner wisdom is the collection of all your experiences, even including those you may have forgotten about but remain recorded in the annals of your memory and the wisdom of your body. It can assess complicated situations in a split second and inform you of your options and which route to take. Like a hotline you can dial whenever you seek advice, it is always ready to help you. In fact, it's waiting patiently for you to recognize its existence and call out for its assistance. Just like a close friend, your intuition is eager to serve its primary purpose: being there for you when you need it most.

What do you say? Isn't it time that you got (re)acquainted? Let me take the liberty of introducing you both.

First of all, every single one of us has our own name for our intuition. We all know what it's like to make contact with this part of us, although, depending on our life experiences and how we define our reality, we will use different terminology. To clarify, while I will mostly revert to the term intuition throughout this book, I'd like to share some other names for this inner superpower we all have access to, based on what I've heard from people over the years. I encourage you to add your own to the list:

- inner sense
- sixth sense
- spidey sense (after the superhero character Spiderman, whose extrasensory perception allows him to sense and respond to threats)
- inner compass
- inner guide
- gut feeling
- hunch
- inner nudge
- inner tickle
- a knowing in your bones

No matter what you choose to call it, your intuition is a powerful complement (and perhaps even amalgamation) of all five of your senses and your natural human capacity to take in and process information. While processing our five senses consciously can be seen as the tip of the iceberg, our intuition has access to the submerged part of the iceberg that we can't necessarily see or make sense of (the unconscious and subconscious mind). Science has verified its existence, although researchers may have their own ways of defining or assessing intuition. When we're in the realm of numbers, measurements, and evidence, intuition can feel a little mystifying and elusive. However, while researchers are helping us understand the scientific basis of it in even more concrete terms, intuition also has an important qualitative dimension that we can start to recognize in practical ways.

This chapter will offer you a solid foundation for understanding the many dimensions of intuition: what the research is bringing to our awareness, as well as how we can start to work with this powerful inner tool. The first section of this chapter details some of the most significant research studies on intuition. For all the science buffs, my hope is that you'll develop a newfound appreciation for the practical understanding of the application of intuition. Of course, if you'd prefer to skip that section to get straight to the personal benefits and ramifications, I encourage you to follow your intuition there!

The Research on Intuition

Scientists in a variety of fields—including psychology, neuroscience, cognitive science, and management science—have been studying intuition for decades. There is consensus that intuition exists as an ability we all have. Some studies go into discussions of how to define intuition and what type of processes are included in it. The main focus of the empirical studies is testing for and evaluating the results of intuition. This can prove challenging, as most of the participants and test subjects are not trained or experienced in tapping into their intuition. Even with that caveat, many studies have still demonstrated solid proof of our intuitive processing capabilities and their benefits.

Here, I'd like to touch on the most influential and groundbreaking studies on intuition, but throughout this book, I'll be dropping in further research as it relates to each specific topic we'll cover.

One of the fundamental things to remember is that intuition is an aspect of our learning. It's tied to a process known as implicit learning—or, in other words, learning by doing. Because implicit learning is focused on activity, we tend to acquire knowledge and skills in this arena without being aware of it. Another aspect of intuition is pattern recognition, which can be rapid or show up after gaining experience.

In the well-known matrix scanning experiment done by Lewicki, Czyzewska, and Hoffman in 1987, participants were asked to detect which of the four quadrants on the computer screen the target number 6 appeared in. They were shown a sequence of seven screens followed by a short break, with the number 6 placed in one of the quadrants in each screen. Their task was to press buttons corresponding to the quadrant of number 6 and do this as quickly as possible. Other numbers were thrown in on the screen to create distractions.

The researchers had built a complex sequencing rule that determined where the number 6 would appear on the seventh screen based on where it was on the previous screens. The participants were not told about this beforehand, and there wasn't any way for them to figure out the formula via conscious analysis. The participants started to correctly detect number 6 after a few trials, and their speed of response for the seventh screen exceeded their speed of response to the sixth screen as if they knew the formula. After practicing for many hours, they became even faster at finding where the target number appeared on the seventh screen. This demonstrated that they had implicitly learned the sequencing rule and figured out the pattern intuitively.

To test their hypothesis, the researchers changed the sequencing rule after a few hours, before restoring it once more. Participants' reaction times in each segment of the experiment reflected that, when the rule was present, they could implicitly follow it, even when they weren't aware of doing so. They were even offered a cash reward for explaining the sequencing rule, but they couldn't! This is because they were following their intuition, not some conscious rationale.

Another influential study on intuition was conducted by Antonio Damasio and his colleagues in 1994. Damasio's seminal study is known as the Iowa Gambling Task. He and his colleagues designed and ran an experiment in which participants chose cards from four card decks. They were told that each card they pulled had game money rewards and penalties. The participants did not know that two of the decks had large rewards and large penalties, whereas the other two decks had smaller rewards and smaller penalties. Two of the decks were generally profitable, while the other two resulted in net losses. The goal of the game was to win as much money as possible. The participants with dysfunction in a specific region of the frontal lobe of their brain, which is involved in decision-making, repeatedly made bad choices. After forty trials, the participants with healthy brain function demonstrated intuitive ability to pick the better decks without being able to explain how. Damasio and his colleagues concluded that intuitive guidance could play a role in decision-making.

In another seminal 1990 study, the late cognitive psychology researcher Kenneth S. Bowers and his colleagues gave word puzzles to their participants. These were word triads, and the goal was to judge whether they were connected (coherent). There was a fourth word that completed the picture and made the connection clear for the triads that were coherent, but the participants were not told what this word was. The research team found that the participants were able to identify the connected word sets even if they could not identify the fourth word which linked them. Bowers and his team concluded that people were able to make connections intuitively without consciously analyzing the components.

Building on that 1990 study, Annette Bolte and her colleague Thomas Goschke did their own word triads puzzle experiment and investigated the response times under different time constraints. The participants were able to solve the puzzles intuitively within two seconds.

The renowned cognitive scientist Gary A. Klein also made significant contributions to intuition research. He studied people who were skilled and experienced in their areas of expertise and looked at how they made decisions, which he referred to as naturalistic decision-making. Klein conducted research on how people deal with and resolve unusual challenges. His book *Sources of Power: How People Make Decisions* offers true accounts of people taking action under extreme time and performance constraints and volatile conditions. He studied firefighters, critical-care nurses, pilots, nuclear power-plant operators, battle planners, and chess masters, and explored how these experts used their intuition and experience to make effective decisions. He focused on people who had considerable experience, meaning they had also substantially accumulated a great deal of unconsciously stored data on various situations, in addition to conscious knowledge.

This nonconscious experience and knowledge base allows intuition to play a significant role in the decisions made by such professionals.

In one of the true stories covered in *Sources of Power*, a firefighter describes a fire he and his crew once fought at the back of a house. They were in the living room, spraying water on the kitchen fire, but the flames kept flaring up. The firefighter had an uneasy feeling that nudged him to get his team out. The living room floor collapsed as they reached the street. The whole team would have fallen into the burning basement if he had not followed his gut feeling. Klein explained that the firefighter's decision was based on recognizing subtle cues, such as the temperature of the living room and the muffled faint sounds of the fire burning in the basement underneath, which didn't match his expectations of a typical kitchen fire. Klein explained that firefighters sometimes make decisions by recognizing patterns and anomalies based on their experience rather than through a process of conscious linear logic.

In 2006, social psychologist Ap Dijksterhuis of Radboud University in the Netherlands, and his colleague Loran Nordgren at Kellogg School of Management, published a seminal research paper proposing unconscious thought theory (UTT). This theory suggests that our unconscious mind is capable of performing complex tasks without our being consciously aware of it. I would call this an intuitive process. The authors add that the unconscious process performs better than conscious thought in making complex decisions involving many variables. The research team ran experiments in which the participants were given choices to make, such as the best car among a set of options. The participants were either allowed to think about which choice to make, or were distracted from this task by having their conscious mind focus on solving unrelated puzzles or discussing other topics. The results showed that the participants who were not allowed to consciously think about which choice to make actually made better decisions when presented with car choices that had many attributes. This implies that unconscious thought processes such as intuition could be helpful in the integration of complex information. Moreover, individuals might benefit from stepping away from information to allow their unconscious mind to process it—which could lead to better outcomes.

In recent years, scientific research on intuition evolved into attempting to identify the components of the intuitive process. Researchers like Thea Zander at the University of Basel and her colleagues defined intuition and insight as two different nonconscious processes that build on each other. They described intuition as a gut feeling or an instinctual response that comes from prior experiences and accumulated knowledge. On the other hand, insight was characterized by a sudden revelation about a situation or a solution to a problem that involved a cognitive leap. I actually consider insight as part of the intuitive process. A more recent study published in 2021 by Paola Adinolfi at the University of Salerno and her colleagues also concluded that intuition encompasses various cognitive processes, including insight.

When it comes to the conditions that allow intuition to work, Joel Pearson, a neuroscientist and professor at the University of South Wales, has some ideas. His 2024 book, *The Intuition Toolkit*, defines intuition as "the learnt, productive use of unconscious information to improve decisions or actions." He uses the acronym SMILE to describe five conditions that need to be satisfied for intuition to work: The letters correspond to:

- S: self-awareness (caution about using intuition when under the influence of high emotions)
- M: mastery (relying on intuition in areas where the person has a lot of experience or expertise)
- I: impulses (knowing the difference between impulses and addictions and intuition)
- L: low probability (not using intuition for low-probability events or situations such as rare occurrences)
- E: environment (using intuition only in familiar and predictable contexts).

A groundbreaking 2016 study conducted by Galang Lufityanto, Chris Donkin, and Joel Pearson demonstrates that not only does intuition exist—but it can also be objectively measured. Participants in this study were asked to solve visual motion puzzles while they were also being exposed to emotional images in one eye to create specific experiences that were either pleasant or unpleasant. The solutions to the visual puzzles were connected to the type of emotion evoked by these images. Participants' conscious memory of these images was erased with flashing lights directed to the other eye, which is a proven scientific technique for suppressing memories of visual images. Skin conductance tests showed that the participants still registered the emotions evoked by the images and recorded these experiences in some way; for example, sweat might appear on participants' bodies if they came in contact with a frightening image. As they attempted to solve the puzzles, they were able to predict the results based on their unconscious memories of the emotions evoked by the images, which provided a key to the solution that was outside their conscious mind. It's a form of pattern recognition that demonstrates the way information gets stored in the unconscious and re-accessed through intuition.

The results showed that the participants successfully integrated and made use of these experiences, even if they did not have any conscious memory of them, in solving the puzzles faster and with higher accuracy and confidence compared to the experiment that excluded the emotional images. This productive use of unconsciously stored information fits the definition of an intuitive process. In addition, the research team also found that, with practice, the participants got better at this intuitive process over time. The research team concluded that "something that resembles the general description of intuition does indeed exist, and can be precisely measured."

As shown in this research paper, part of our intuition comes from the accumulation of experiences and our reactions to them that are stored in our nonconscious mind and neurological system including our gut and heart. We are bombarded with vast amounts of information and data every day. Our brain captures some of this and stores it in the conscious so that we can pull out the necessary information when we need to. Intuition functions as our internal search engine that can access all that information including the conscious, subconscious, and unconscious (considered to be deeper and less readily available than subconscious) without expending overwhelming amounts of energy and effort. On top of its amazing data retrieval, intuition also runs probability calculations and weighs each possible outcome against each other to—bing!—come up with an answer in a split second, or in some cases all of a sudden, after leaving the problem unattended for a while.

Even people who say they have no intuition whatsoever can find examples of this inner wisdom at play in their lives if they look for it carefully. Asserting that we have no intuition is pretty much the same thing as saying that we have no emotions or thoughts. As long as we are in good mental health, and we're not feeling numb from a big shock, emotions are always running through us, and thoughts and ideas are constantly circling in our minds. Physiological changes occur in our bodies in response to these emotions and thoughts. Hormones are released and sensations ask for our attention. Intuition is also capable of using this inner body language to warn us of potential dangers or to excite us about the imminent arrival of good news.

We typically think of our five basic senses when we consider sensations, but we can still neglect some of the signals from these senses in the rush to get through our endless to-do lists. Our sense of smell can be quiet until an extreme trigger, such as smoke from something burning, wakes it up. We may not notice all the constant low-volume sounds around us until we need to pay attention to an unusual noise coming from outside. Intuition can also easily take the back seat and practically put itself on mute until we decide to invite it to the front row of our lives.

Inviting intuition to take its seat in our daily lives is becoming easier, especially since research on intuition has evolved significantly over the last few decades. Scientists went from attempting to figure out how to define intuition to actually accepting it as a fact; from exploring the conditions under which intuition works best to devising methods of quantitatively measuring it in a laboratory environment. At the same time, it's important to note that there is no final consensus about intuition in the scientific community; thus, it's unlikely that we'll have some kind of grand unified theory of intuition to answer all our questions. After all, a number of researchers from diverse disciplines are studying intuition, which means there is still a great deal of debate over what it is.

One of my hopes in particular is that, with the growing number of empirical studies about intuition, more scientists will account for participants who are already well-trained in using their intuition—not just for simple decision-making but perhaps also in more complex situations. In chapter 3, you will learn about what it means to prime for intuition—which refers to re-creating, as closely as possible, the environment and the mental and emotional state our intuition thrives in. I can't help but wonder: If scientists were to repeat their studies but prime their subjects beforehand, how would this inform a more empirical understanding of intuition?

Although many questions remain to be answered, as science continues to refine our general understanding of intuition, as well as how and when it works well, it is possible that we will come closer to a more mainstream acceptance of this powerful force—and how we can access it to our advantage.

Why Is Intuition Important?

In addition to the debate over the definition of intuition in scientific research, various dictionaries also differ in the wording or details. The Merriam-Webster Dictionary says that it is "the power or faculty of attaining to direct knowledge or cognition without evident rational thought and inference." The Cambridge Dictionary explains intuition as "(knowledge from) an ability to understand or know something immediately based on your feelings rather than facts." Regardless of the variations, it is widely agreed that intuition is our inner wisdom that guides us in decisions and helps us create ideas and find solutions to our problems without the need for conscious analysis.

What I and many other people have discovered is that expanding our awareness to include intuition enriches our lives. We get to see situations and problems from other angles. As our awareness grows, so does our capacity to live with greater wisdom and clarity. Getting in touch with our intuition helps us become more resourceful, relaxed, compassionate, and empathetic. Intuition can also help us navigate conflict and communicate more smoothly in our relationships. When we're having a difficult conversation or find ourselves in a challenging situation, intuiting the other person's emotional state can be extremely effective. Our intuition can guide us about the best words to say, or it might tell us to just be patient and quiet, and listen—to whatever is spoken, as well as unspoken. For example, wouldn't it be wonderful if you could sense that your teammate is going through a difficult transition in his life that would explain his erratic behavior of late? For partners and spouses, you could probably imagine a myriad of ways in which a deeper knowing about your partner's current state of emotions could be of benefit to both of you. Intuition is a powerful tool, especially when more direct communication is tricky or, in some cases, not even possible.

I've certainly met introspective students who have asked me, "How do I know that acting on my intuition isn't just the same as acting on biases I'm not aware of?"

As you'll learn in the next chapter, a major characteristic of intuition is nonjudgmental openness—and in general, openness and bias don't go hand-in-hand. Intuition invites you to explore, learn, investigate, and let it all simmer before you make any final judgments or decisions. It helps you question your conclusions, face your prejudices, and trace them back to their source. As you'll learn in this book, you can use intuition to discover where your biases are, and with that awareness, take steps toward positive change.

Going through life with your intuition alive and active is like using your side- and rearview mirrors when driving. It can give you perspective and remind you of all the experience and knowledge you've accumulated that can be daunting for your conscious thoughts to sift through. Intuition helps you see things from different angles and notice that which you may not have been able to perceive with conscious analysis.

Making Better Decisions with Intuition

One of the most frequently asked questions by my students and clients is how to make decisions that incorporate intuition. They wonder, "What if my intuition is wrong, and I make the wrong decision based on my so-called hunch?" What so many people tend to forget or not realize is that intuition is one of many inputs we need to make sound decisions. In addition to intuition, we should also be taking our logic, research, and expert opinions into account.

We can start to utilize our intuition to effective ends by realizing that it tries to speak to us in many ways, but it doesn't have a specific language. For some people, intuition can pop up as images in their mind—or, in other words, in their mind's eye. For others, it may be a word or words that come seemingly out of nowhere. There are also people who feel intuition as a sensation in their body, such as a warmth in the chest or heart area.

When these messages from our intuition show up in our minds as images, strings of words, or sensations in the body, we are accustomed to translating them into words we can understand. As a result, some valuable input from our intuition can be lost in translation, in the same way we might interpret a dream the following morning but leave out any tidbits that don't fit our interpretation, based on how we've come to habitually process certain symbols and bits of information. For example, if our intuition is trying to deliver the message to take it slow or be cautious in a situation, we can interpret it as "Don't go that way" or "Stay away from that." Our interpretation of our intuition may be off, or there could also be the possibility that our intuition itself is totally off. The experience and knowledge stored in our subconscious or unconscious may not be sufficient for our intuition to tap into for a reliable conclusion, or we may be applying what's there to the wrong context.

Imagine an old-fashioned filing drawer with many different files. Perhaps the information we require needs to come from a file we don't actually have—so our intuition grabs the next best file, even though it doesn't quite fit our situation. This is why it's a good idea to use intuition as only one input in our decision-making! We usually seek advice from many sources before we make important decisions. For example, if we are considering a life-changing decision, we don't only talk to one friend or only one family member about it. When we are buying a car, ideally, we don't go to just one car dealer and test-drive only one car. We gather information, ask around, get input, ponder it, sleep on it, then make a decision.

Bringing intuition into your life is as simple as adding one more input source into your research before you make a decision. You still need to consider different viewpoints, as well as your own calculations and logical deductions, and compare all of that to what your intuition says. If your intuition agrees, the decision is easy. If your intuition disagrees with the results of all your research efforts, it may be telling you to do some more digging and asking around, or it may be signaling that the decision is right, but the timing may be wrong.

Your intuition can also act like a safety check. It can slow you down to look around again, which may be a good thing. Intuition is not about being right or wrong; sometimes, the mere feeling that something is off is enough to make us look again and reconsider the facts and factors.

In addition, your gut feeling is not only about yes versus no. It can be saying, "Maybe, but it will be messy," or, "Yes, but not yet," or, "No, but keep watching all the factors involved to catch the right time."

Sometimes, all our resources will agree and point to one sharply focused bull's-eye. Everything clicks and makes sense, and we know what to do. Sometimes, our intuition may tell us the opposite of what everyone else and our own analysis of the situation say. In those cases, we can go back to our intuition to check in again and ask for more clarification or insights into the situation. Then, we can look to our other inputs or factors and see if we missed anything. Maybe the direction can be slightly changed for everything to fit together. It may also be that the timing of the action is not quite right, and this rethinking gives us the additional time we need to be comfortable with making our decision. At the end of the day, good decision-making means that all of us need to run all the factors through the filter of logic and intellect before deciding what to do. Intuition and intellect are complements, not competitors. We can use them in tandem.

My friend Sally always had the hunch that she needed to live in Norway for a while before she settled anywhere else after college, even though she'd never been to Norway before. When she was close to college graduation, she researched all her options, and talked to anyone she could find who had been to Norway or was from there. All the information she gathered took her in the direction of Norway, so she didn't hesitate—she packed her bags and moved there. In her case, her intuition agreed with all the other factors she took into consideration, which made her decision easy. It was a huge step in her life, but she had no confusion whatsoever.

One of my intuitive guidance clients, Diana, had to deal with the confusion of her intellect not matching her intuition around the time when she and her husband were looking for a house to buy. After going to open houses for about a year, they saw one they both liked. The location was great, the inspection report seemed to offer good marks without any red flags, and making their offer went smoothly. However, there was something that kept nagging at Diana. She described it as a feeling that something wasn't quite right, even if everything and everyone were telling her not to miss this opportunity. She and her husband decided to continue their search. A few months later, they found out that the house was undergoing major repairs, as some structural damage had been omitted from the inspection report.

Since we're on the topic of choosing a place to live—whether that means a particular geographic location or a home—I'd like to share my experience, which is counter to Diana's. When my husband and I decided to purchase a house in the San Francisco Bay Area many years ago, it felt like everything came together with the utmost ease. But, as soon as everything suddenly became "real," my intuition felt heavy; I could sense that it was telling me "something is not right!" However, all our friends, including some who were Realtors, insisted that now was the right time. If we didn't get into the housing market at this moment, as things were becoming increasingly competitive, it might never happen. Logic and research were telling us to go for it, but my intuition was insisting the opposite. What to do? It was a difficult moment, but I did my best to sit quietly and discern whether my intuition was saying "Don't do it!" or just warning me to "Go ahead but be cautious."

In the end, after weighing my options, I went with logic. Today, I'm so grateful I did! In retrospect, I recognize that my intuition wasn't literally telling me not to purchase the house; rather, it was cluing me in to the fact that, because it was an older building, there would be a lot of time, effort, and money spent on repairs and renovations—in other words, it would be a painful process. All these years later, I'm so happy I wasn't deterred by that sense of warning. In fact, I know that taking on the challenge of home repairs actually strengthened my patience and resilience.

Ultimately, the decision as to whether or not you should rely on your intuition depends on how costly it would be if you turned out to be wrong. In small decisions, in which the cost of being wrong isn't too high, I suggest following your intuition and seeing where it takes you. First, make sure that there is no risk of harm for you or anyone else; you can do this by running the potential decision through the filter of your reasoning and intellect. If there is no danger, it can be fun to try out what your intuition says and see how it goes. Make a low-stakes decision using your intuitive guidance; go to an ice-cream shop and try a new flavor just by relying on your intuition. Trying one scoop of the butterscotch raspberry parfait is unlikely to hurt you, if you are not allergic to any of the ingredients of course.

If there's a high cost to your intuition being wrong, such as potential harm to you or someone else, then you can avoid taking the risk and go with your logic and intellect instead. People performing extreme sports might completely disagree with this—for many of them, the contact high of achieving what nobody else has managed to outweighs the possibility of a potential injury. Still, if you feel like trying hang-gliding, even if it's the tandem version with a very experienced professional, it's best to think before you act and consider all risks carefully rather than blaming your intuition afterward.[1]

You can ask your intuition what the answer is for something before you look up information or do research on the topic, but once you get used to recognizing your intuition, you can use it anytime—even after you've done research and received other people's input. When you are first practicing, it's easier to consult with your intuition before muddling it with any other input. Remember—you will still consider all input before making the decision.

This is where I offer the caveat that following your intuition is never about making impulsive snap decisions, although many people confuse the two. Nor is it about letting the voice of fear and extreme caution stop you from taking risks. Intuition is a nonconscious process that taps into all our knowledge and experiences, so it is far from mindless decision-making or random guessing. But again, understanding how to attune to our intuition can take time and practice. If we look at intuition as one of many factors to take into account in making a decision, then still run the proposed decision through our intellect, we reduce the chances of running into problems!

When to Trust Your Intuition

Related to the question of how we can use our intuition to tap into good decision-making, clients often ask me, "How do I know it's my intuition talking? What if it's just my conscious

---

[1] Here, I want to emphasize that if you are in a situation where there are major risks in any direction you choose to take, and you are facing a clear and imminent danger (such as a toxic relationship), it is important to seek out professional help and support.

mind, full of its judgments and prejudices?" The answer to this one is both easy and difficult.

First, it's best to check in with your intuition right away when you have a decision to make or a question you would like guidance on. Tune in to your intuition before gathering data and thinking about the issue. This way, it's easier to identify the intuitive message. If you ponder the issue and do research about it and talk to people, your mind will likely be filled with the conclusions or confusion you gather from all those resources. Then, when you try to tune in to your intuition, it may be muddled by all the information you already have. If you ask your intuition first, and you receive an answer that is fear-based, a worst-case scenario, or could harm you or anyone else, you can pretty much cross it off your list. Intuition is kind and does not paint detailed worst-case scenarios that strike fear in our hearts. If the message is gentle, encouraging, subtle, and would not harm you or anyone else, then it is most likely your intuition speaking.

I always stress to my clients that tuning in to our intuition isn't the same as acting on it. You have free will and can consciously choose what you wish to do. It is healthy to question your intuition and not just trust any hunch you get without discernment. Over time, as you consult with your intuition more often, you'll learn how to receive its particular guidance, without doubting its presence, and combine it with your intellect.

I often find that my clients feel more comfortable using their intuition when they are reminded that it is a natural part of us—and we all have it. When we're tapping into it, we're not connecting to a magical source that's correct 100 percent of the time; rather, we're communing more fully with the world and the universe around us. We have many other natural abilities, such as conscious or logical thinking, but we don't say that all our thoughts are correct! We don't give up on thinking because sometimes our thoughts turn out to be incorrect. We are so used to having thoughts and using and living with them that conscious thinking is part of the natural flow of our day—and we can exercise discernment when it comes to deciding whether or not to act on it.

In some situations when you are trying to make a decision with your conscious mind, the picture may be too blurry, and your intuition can help shine some light on it. In other situations, intuition can paint a missing color into the scene that makes all other factors fit better together. Sometimes, the big picture is too much for our conscious thinking to wrap around it. There may be too many moving parts, too much history, and so on. In such cases, intuition can be very helpful and give us a sense of direction.

Intuition sometimes gets our attention turned in a direction that we may have missed before and would not even think of looking at if we hadn't tapped into our inner guidance in the first place. When we explore this new direction, we can ask our intuition for further guidance.

My client Susan had two academic job offers she was considering. They were both good offers, with one having clear advantages over the other. Her logic said to accept that one right away. When she tapped into her intuition about these places, she wasn't excited about either of them. This made her ask for more time to consider the offers and follow up with some other potential jobs she had interviewed for. One of the universities that she had given up on, since she had not heard from them in a while, told her to come in for another round of interviews. She got to see the town and the nearby big city when she traveled there, and she instantly fell in love with the location. When she received the offer, her decision was clear. In this case, Susan felt that her intuition was directing her toward a possibility that hadn't been on the table. Because she was patient and willing to remain in uncertainty a bit longer rather than make a decision instantaneously, she received more information that led to a positive outcome.

Again, asking if you should trust your intuition is just like asking if you should trust your thoughts. Intuition is just one of our abilities, and just like conscious thinking, it needs to be questioned, contextualized, and compared to other sources.

Discerning whether to trust your thoughts would depend on many factors. How solid and reliable do those thoughts feel? Are they based on subjective judgments and opinions or on facts? How much conscious thinking or analysis has gone into them? How much research preceded them?

The same goes for intuition. When you received an intuitive "hit," what was your emotional state? How active was your conscious thinking in the moment? How solid does your intuition feel when you quiet down your mind chatter and relax long enough to check in with it to see if it changes?

In the end, it's up to us to use all our abilities and capabilities to their full extent. In addition, instead of merely relying on our personal logic and intellect, it's a good idea to check all of this against other people's guidance, especially if they are experts or more experienced in that area.

Although my work is all about getting people in touch

with their intuition, I still offer my clients the caveat that sometimes we try to read too much into our intuition. We try to analyze and judge it, based on what we think we know. We try to decipher the message until it's set in stone. Often, it might be simpler than we're trying to make it. Many times, all our intuition is saying, when translated into conscious thinking and language, is, "Pay attention here."

One of the keys to using and practicing with your intuition is learning not to be so attached to the outcome. If you follow your intuition after running it through the filter of your logic and everything turns out great, that's wonderful. On the other hand, if you follow your intuition and things don't quite work out the way you hoped, you can still learn something from that experience. You may have interpreted your intuition incorrectly, or the circumstances and people involved in that situation changed to alter the results, or your intuition might have been off. In the cases where you didn't follow your intuition and it turned out to be a mistake, you can still ask yourself and your intuition what you can learn from that experience. Please remember that the growth and lessons gained from the process of working with your intuition are extremely powerful in and of themselves.

How Does Intuition Communicate with Us?

As I mentioned earlier, our intuition can communicate with us in a number of ways. At the same time, we are all unique individuals who sense intuition differently.

Some people describe a gut feeling, whereas others have a knowing or thought that appears seemingly out of nowhere.

Some people hear sounds, see pictures, or even smell odors when their intuition is at work.

My clients and students report many different ways in which their intuition communicates with them. One of the questions they ask early in our lessons and consultation sessions is how to know the difference between their fears and their intuition when they sense a warning. The flip side of this is distinguishing between their wishes or dreams and intuition in the case of receiving a positive message.

The main identifying component of our intuition is that it suddenly pops into our head or nudges us with sensations, without any conscious chain of thought preceding it. Intuitive messages are also usually gentle and subtle. When a student, client, or a friend tells me about nightmarish scenarios they had in their imagination and asks if those were their intuition speaking, I remind them that intuition delivers a quick message and does not continue to write a whole horror story. Usually, the conscious mind takes over after a warning from our intuition and writes the scenarios in detail for us!

Now, let's look a little more at how our intuition delivers its often subtle messages and communicates with us in a variety of ways:

- **Through our five senses:** Intuitive messages can come from our vision, hearing, smell, taste, and sense of touch. For example, we might hear a song in our head, see a picture in our mind's eye, get a taste (or memory of a taste) in our mouth, suddenly feel cold or warm, or experience sensations in our body, almost as if something brushed over us.

- **Through sensations inside the body:** This is also known as interoception and can show up in a myriad of ways—as a gut feeling or a weight in the belly, a sped-up heart rate, tightness or fluttering in the chest, a warmth or coldness in the limbs, or tingling inside different parts of the body.
- **Through cognition:** This is usually described as knowing something without any idea of how you came to know it. Sometimes, words or ideas might arise to offer us insights on where to go or what to do.
- **Through unexplained emotions:** These can include sudden feelings of sadness or joy, or an emotion of unease that cannot be tied to a specific reason or source. Although these emotions may come on suddenly, they are usually subtle and nondramatic. It is valuable to notice and record them; when more information is available, you might look back on your notes and realize they were relevant.
- **Through dialogue:** This one usually surprises my students. You can actually ask questions and listen to your intuition with all your senses and awareness to receive answers in various forms. You can interview your intuition the way talk show hosts interview their guests. We'll get into methods of conversing with your inner guidance throughout this book.

One of my students, Oya, told me that she used to feel her intuition physically, through her gut. She was a personal trainer who loved to move and exercise, so it made sense for the language of her intuition to be conveyed through physical sensations around her core, which is considered to be the power center of the body. In the last few years, her life transformed so that she now does less physical work and has more heart-to-heart communications with clients and colleagues. She also began to volunteer and work with children, which increased her sense of living from her heart. Thus, it was not surprising when she told me that her sense of where her intuition was located had shifted to her heart.

Many of us, at least for a time, tend to connect to one particular way of accessing our intuition more than others, although it varies for everyone. Like Oya, you might find that your inner sense speaks to you in a different way at different stages of life. I also want to emphasize that, while we tend to be a visually focused culture, many books on intuition will emphasize "visualizing" scenarios in our mind's eye; this doesn't work for everyone. If you're not a visual person, you can also sense, feel, hear, or know your intuition in ways that work for you.

Exercise: Journal Your Intuition

The first homework assignment I give all my intuition students and clients is to journal about their experiences of making contact with their intuition. It is highly informative and useful to write down or record any intuitive experiences you notice throughout your day. I like to use a physical journal that I can write longhand in, but you can also use your phone or any other device. If it is not feasible to do this during the day, you can allocate a few minutes to recording these incidents before going to bed every night so you can capture what you remember from the day and possibly previous days if you haven't recorded your intuitive experiences for some time. However, I recommend making a habit of noting intuitive moments when they happen, as much as you can. Intuition is a lot like dreams—when we don't capture an experience with our full awareness, it has a higher likelihood of fading.

When you journal your intuition, you create your own intuition database. You need to include details such as the time of the day you had the intuition, your emotional state at that time, your environment, and other details you can capture that seem relevant. Gathering data on how your intuition functions is very important. It allows you to learn more about the inner workings of your intuition—as well as potentially optimal moments for close contact with your intuition.

Each person's inner wisdom works in its own way, and you can obtain unique insights about the kinds of conditions that make your intuition more active when you gather data through journaling. As you accumulate this detailed information, you also start to figure out how you can prepare yourself and modify your environment to allow your intuition to communicate with you more frequently and clearly. For example, you might discover that you can hear that small, still voice within when you take time to meditate early in the morning, or when you go on a daily run that allows you to put aside worries and concerns.

Your intuition may bring brilliant ideas and nudges in the right direction. It may also give you clear messages not to do something. Even if you eventually decide to ignore that feeling, record the fact that you had such an inkling, because it may be relevant and informative down the line. Also record what day and time it was, what kind of mood you were in, where you were, who was there with you, and any other details of your environment, such as whether it was quiet or noisy. You can use the following template if it's helpful:

Date:

Time of Day:

Mood/Emotional State:

Location:

Who I Was With:

Environment (indoors or outdoors, weather, temperature, noise level, activity level, overall vibe, etc.):

Intuitive Insights That Came to Me:

How They Came to Me (e.g., "I heard a voice in my head that reminded me of a person I haven't spoken to in years, which was unexpected"; "I had a feeling that I needed to turn around and take a different path to get to my destination"):

How I Felt About Them (e.g., curious, confused, happy, inspired, etc.):

Key Takeaways

- Your intuition is a powerful complement (and perhaps even amalgamation) of all five of your senses and your natural human capacity to take in and process information—and it goes by many different names.

- There is scientific consensus that intuition exists as an ability we all have. Many studies have demonstrated solid proof of our intuitive processing capabilities and their benefits.
- Intuition can be powerful in helping us make decisions because it helps us see things from different angles and notice that which we may not have been able to perceive with conscious analysis.
- Intuition tries to speak to us in many ways, but it doesn't have a specific language. For some people, intuition can pop up as images in their mind, words, sensations, or an inexplicable knowing.
- Ultimately, the decision as to whether or not you should rely on your intuition depends on how costly it would be if you turned out to be wrong. In small decisions, in which the cost of being wrong isn't too high, you can test following your intuition and see where it takes you.
- It is always healthy to question your intuition, run it through your logic, compare to other inputs, and not merely go with any hunch you get without discernment.
- Many of us connect to one particular way of accessing our intuition more than others, and we may also find that our inner sense speaks to us in a different way at different stages of life.
- Journaling your intuition can help create your own intuition database, which is a valuable resource that helps you build your awareness of how your intuition works and under what circumstances.

Reflections

- Do you have a special name for your intuition? If so, what is it?
- When do you naturally tend to tune in to your intuition?
- Do you believe intuition is something that can be quantified or measured? What makes this so?
- Does your intuition communicate with you in a particular way or through different channels?
- Under which conditions do you notice your intuition becoming more active?
- Was there a time when you clearly noticed your intuition saying one thing and your logic saying something else? How did you resolve this seeming conflict? In retrospect, how do you feel about it?

CHAPTER 2

Beyond Conscious Thinking—The Characteristics of Intuition

I hope you have already begun to put your intuition into practice and to keep a running log of your intuitive encounters. This process is extremely important in helping you work with your intuition, but it's also necessary to recognize the primary characteristics of intuition to tell it apart from your conscious thoughts. There's nothing wrong with conscious thoughts—in fact, as I've already mentioned, we need to rely on both our intuition and our logical, reasoning mind to make well-informed decisions. However, too many people confuse their intuition with their logical analysis, fears, judgments, or wishes, which can skew their relationship to their intuition, as well as their ability to capture it.

Recognizing your intuition can be a little challenging initially, but it gets easier over time as you gain more experience. Your understanding of intuition evolves, and you get better at recognizing and accessing it whenever you need. Just like learning to work with a new teammate, you may not know how to communicate at first. You might stumble and make mistakes, but over time, you establish an interpersonal rhythm that ensures your collaboration is productive.

In this chapter, we'll explore the primary characteristics of intuition, which will offer you valuable insight that will enable you to better answer the question: "Is this my intuition talking—or is it something else?"

Intuition Is a Part of You

Before we dive into the many characteristics of intuition, I want to discuss implicit learning and its connection to intuition, as this will help you understand and appreciate the way intuition works—and how it is likely occurring in the background of your life without your awareness or appreciation.

One of the common forms of intuitive processes is implicit learning, a type of learning that occurs when our conscious mind isn't directly involved. Our lives are filled with many examples of this. That means we all practice intuition without even realizing it. There are many daily functions that we engage in on autopilot (for example, typing, showering, or driving). We just perform them—and if necessary, we modify them intuitively in the moment.

Implicit learning is also known as learning by doing—or in some cases, muscle memory, because we are observing what is happening with every part of our body. We record every detail in our unconscious and subconscious mind and neurological system through the nerves going into every part of our body, without even trying to do so. That's why we can repeat the process when necessary but can't even explain how we do it if asked. Implicit learning can be an important component of intuition in some cases, but it does not encompass all intuitive processes. Intuition can also include other nonconscious tasks, such as rapid pattern recognition and an uncanny ability to assess the likelihood of various outcomes. Implicit learning can easily fall apart if the conditions are stable but suddenly change, which reduces our chances of reproducing success; in contrast, if intuition is trained and involved, it can sense and recognize the change in conditions and alert us so we can make necessary adjustments.

There are many instances of intuition that overlap with implicit learning and our intuitive ability actually assists and enhances our implicit learning. One example is a baby who is learning to walk. No one tells the baby to first lift one foot, then put it down a bit in front of them, then move their body weight onto that foot and lift the other foot while bringing it a bit more forward—all while paying attention to the surface they're walking on and obstacles around them, as they maintain focus on their target destination. As babies (and even in adulthood, after an injury), we learn how to walk intuitively. Some researchers would call this implicit learning, but I believe that there's the additional intuitive benefit of calculation of possibilities here. Babies are able to assess a new environment and perform this newly acquired skill surprisingly well, even if they wobble. When babies start to walk, they are extremely good at adapting to changing conditions very quickly. Their eyes scan the environment like a robot vacuum before they take another step. They do a much better job than the robot vacuum that runs an algorithm in its computer to assess the new surface texture and obstacles. I believe there is an extremely complicated algorithm running in babies' minds, too, but it is a nonconscious process that doesn't overwhelm them. Without intuition at play here, the baby or toddler could keep falling down and give up or have a temper tantrum.

Learning to recognize, access, and use intuition is like learning how to walk. In our intuition sessions, I guide my students through examples of how they can remove all obstacles in their way to access their inner wisdom. This involves clearing the mind and calming their emotions. If they have a question, they can drop it into that calmness and stillness, which fills both their mind and body, and wait for a response. There is some hand-holding, especially in the beginning so that they don't feel discouraged or scared. However, I do not have a key to the wonderful treasure chest of their intuition. Only they do and can discover, or sometimes rediscover, how to open it through practicing tapping into their intuition. The same is true for you.

Those who believe they have no intuition are usually just not aware of all the implicit learning they have acquired throughout their life, which is an intuitive process. Sometimes they face a problem in an area where they have already accumulated a great deal of implicit learning, but since they're used to thinking about a problem in detail, they go into heavy thinking and analyzing. They can instead relax and quiet their conscious thinking, which can bring forth the implicit learning and lead them to a breakthrough. We can all relate to having great ideas or solutions to problems in these kinds of states—when we are simply going on a walk or staring at the sky and clouds, feeling relaxed, our mind still and empty, without trying to figure anything out.

As you learn to catch the times when you have intuitive messages or feelings, through noticing and keeping track, as with the journaling we explored in chapter 1, you are also learning how you receive such messages or images. You are discovering what makes your soil fertile for intuitive seeds to grow.

Intuition Is Gentle

Many clients and students ask me if scary scenarios that pop up in their minds or nightmares are their intuition in action. I maintain that intuition is typically gentle. It is the productive result of our mind sifting through years of unconsciously stored experience and knowledge to come up with a thought or idea to guide us. Our conscious thinking is usually the one that will take an intuitive hunch and build a scary story out of it. Please note that we are not talking about a premonition during which a person has a vision of an accident before it happens. This kind of experience fits the definition of a psychic phenomenon and is outside the scope of this book. What we are focusing on here is the daily practical use of the intuitive ability we all have.

Intuition Is Fun

Many of my students and clients discover that their journey into intuition opens them up to all kinds of fun adventures. They will often wonder aloud, "Why did I wait so late to become friends with my intuition? I'm having the time of my life!"

When you recognize and engage with your intuition, even mundane tasks can turn in to fun activities that you're taking part in with your best friend. When you make friends with your intuition, you can invite it along on tiny and epic adventures. Even grocery shopping can become an interesting practice field for your intuition. When you have questions about what to buy or if you should purchase this or that, you can consult your intuition.

A simple way to do this is to hold the item you are considering buying and ask, "Is this right for me to purchase?" You can even imagine having your intuition speak through the object (more on this later) and ask, "Would you like to come home with me?" This may sound rather silly, but you will be amazed to see how many times you get answers.

Intuition Can Feel Obvious

One of the reasons many people might think their intuition isn't working or may be dormant is that, many times, our intuition tells us things we already know. This is why I tell my clients in their first intuitive guidance sessions that it is very likely I will say things they already know but may just need to hear from someone else.

When people learn to recognize their intuition and access it on demand, they may find that some of the information or guidance matches what they already knew deep down but just haven't fully acknowledged or admitted to themselves. Just as hearing what you already know deep down from someone else can shake you up and give you the jolt you needed, your own intuition can also nudge you in the necessary direction.

For example, a person who is in a job that doesn't match their skill set, utilize their knowledge or experience, or help them grow usually knows it is time to look for another job. However, they might only act on it when a trusted friend or family member says the same thing to them emphatically. So, one of our goals in learning to access our intuition is to have this internal friend who will give us that jolt when we need it.

Intuition Is Direct

Intuition doesn't beat around the bush. It gives its message directly, and that message is typically the first thing that pops into our minds or the first sensation we get after setting the intention of tuning in to a situation, such as dropping a question into the stillness of our mind. It is crucial to catch the first thing that comes to our awareness when we are practicing tapping into our intuition. In cases where intuition shows up by itself without us calling on it, we need to be aware and alert enough to catch the first idea, thought, or sensation that comes up, which may be very subtle.

The first thing that pops up in your mind can be an image, vision, words, sounds, or body sensation. What comes after these initial responses are usually the stories or scenarios that your conscious thinking composes. In such cases, you can still go back and retrieve your original intuition via a technique I call the delete, delete, delete method, which you'll learn about later in this chapter.

Intuition Is Often Subtle

Just as there is a science of intuition, which we covered in chapter 1, there is also an art of intuition. The art of our intuitive ability lies in the capacity to pick up on nuances. Yes, intuition is direct, but that doesn't necessarily mean we will automatically interpret what it's saying to us. Sometimes, our intuition clearly points to a solution, and sometimes it speaks to us in more subtle ways. We may feel a slight skip in our heart, or a quiet nudge in the belly or gut. It can show up as a symbol or metaphor (more on these in a later chapter), or it can bring up a single word that keeps swirling in our awareness. The art of intuition is in how we interpret these subtle signals.

My client Rosa was about to sign a contract with a company. She did her research and talked to everyone she knew who had any information about the organization. She thought about it for days and made her decision. Just when she was about to put her signature on the contract, she had the image of a night light in the shape of the new moon. She was surprised, as this reminded her of the bedside lamp she'd had during her childhood and teenage years. She took a few minutes and did a breathing exercise to quiet her thoughts and get into a calm state so that she could better access her intuition. She wanted to make sure this image was not some random distraction that might cause her to postpone signing the contract. She checked in with her intuition again and asked what she should do.

This time, in her mind's eye, Rosa saw herself sleeping peacefully in her childhood bed. Of course, such an image could have many interpretations. It could mean, "Never sign this contract." It could also mean, "Sleep on it and see how you feel about it tomorrow," or, "Continue to pause and relax, then consider signing later." Rosa could have also interpreted it as, "Sign right now and sleep peacefully, since you will have made the right decision."

Rosa contemplated these possibilities and contacted the company to ask for more time to think about their offer. They gave her a few more days and actually came back with a better offer, since they really needed her and worried that she was second-guessing the offer. She signed the contract and had a good experience working there.

Intuition Is Persistent

Sometimes, when you ask your intuition a question, you may get an answer that you are not so sure of. In these cases, you can quickly drop back in and ask one more time. It is OK to test your intuition! If what you got the first time was from your intuition, it will typically give the same answer when you ask again. Intuition anchors itself, whereas our conscious thoughts tend to change more easily. For example, you ask your intuition a yes or no question, such as "Should I go to the concert tonight?" After you quiet your conscious thoughts and calm your emotions, you receive a no. You can do whatever is needed to drop back into your calm, still mental and emotional state and ask again; see if the no persists.

I refer to this as the shaking-the-answer method. If you have ever seen the magic eight balls that were popular a few decades ago, you might understand why I call it that. Magic eight balls were black pool balls with little windows that showed the words yes, no, maybe, and other responses when you shook them. I give my students this image and tell them to shake the ball and see if the answer they receive is the same as what they received the first time. Typically, when we have a decision to make in complicated or uncertain situations, our conscious thinking can give us different answers each time we think about it. Intuition, on the other hand, will typically give you an answer that stands the shaking test. Again, as I will keep repeating, you need to run what your intuition says through your logic before making an important decision.

Intuition Is Nonjudgmental

Our conscious mind is extremely good at labeling situations, people, places, and events as good or bad. Our inner critic, also referred to as the judge in some coaching styles, is always present and vocal about how things should be and how many things in our lives fit that criteria. We go to a restaurant for the first time and immediately start evaluating what we notice: pretty place, nice and friendly staff, good food, and so on—or the opposite. Early in our lives, we learn to judge from our parents and the other people who have a role in raising us. Many of the criticisms we receive boil down to good versus bad, and we then tend to apply this to everything in our lives.

Intuition, on the other hand, is observant, curious, and open-minded. It still guides us but with blameless discernment rather than the kind of judgment that applies labels and strict rules to our experience. Through our intuitive discernment, going to a new restaurant would render observations like, "What an interesting experience. Staff seem tired—they may have worked long hours today. The food tastes like it was made with care, though," On the less-positive but still more nuanced side, you might get something like, "I have a strange feeling about this place, as if my stomach is saying, 'Don't eat here,' or, 'Choose something plain and small to try first.' I might go with the latter option and see how that works out."

Intuition Lives in the Moment, Unattached to Outcomes

One of the keys to learning to use and practice intuition is being diligent. This is why I emphasize the importance of running your intuition by your logic and other inputs. At the same time, it's a good idea never to get overly attached to outcomes.

One of my students, Fiona, created a spreadsheet of her intuitive experiences after I shared with her the intuition journaling exercise from chapter 1. She had created a column for the outcome, where she graded each entry as "success" or "failure," even though we'd discussed how this way of looking at her intuition might derail her. However, being a self-described type-A person, she was very much under the influence of her hyper-achiever mindset and patterns.

After a certain number of "failures," she decided that her intuition was no good and gave up on learning about it, attempting to notice it in action, and practicing to intentionally tune in to it. I heard from her a year later. She was in crisis mode, as her career and relationships with her family and friends seemed to be falling apart. Ruminating on her problems made matters worse. She was stressed and in desperate need of inner guidance and peace. We resumed our sessions where we'd left off. This time, she was willing to approach practicing intuition with a growth mindset that focused on learning and acknowledged that powerful lessons often come through perceived "failure." Gradually, and with patience, Fiona started to recover her relationships and rebuild her career, as she understood herself and others better. She learned to give herself, the people in her life, and her intuition a second chance.

If you follow your intuition and everything turns out great, that's wonderful. But if you follow your intuition and things don't quite work out the way you would like, there are a few possibilities. It may be the case that the outcome you don't like is what you're meant to go through to learn something—as Fiona figured out was true for herself. In addition, you may have interpreted your intuition incorrectly, your intuition itself might be off, or the circumstances and people involved may have changed after you tuned in. Also, if you don't follow your intuition and you metaphorically fall flat on your face, you can just get up and ask your logic and intuition what you can learn from this experience.

Intuition Is Forgiving

"What happens when I don't follow my intuition and then realize that I should have once the events unfold?" my clients and students often ask me. I reply that life is a continuous learning experience. As long as there is no harm to anyone, you cannot really go wrong; the most important factor at hand is your willingness to learn from every encounter. If you ignore your intuition and then find out you should have listened to it, your intuition will not punish you; it's like a loving parent or a teacher who has your best interests in mind and heart. But sometimes, because they don't know any better, parents or teachers may keep reminding us of our failures. Thankfully, our intuition does not operate that way. It will not repudiate you with a "You should have listened to me!" or "I told you so!" Your intuition will keep holding you gently, and it will be grateful that you noticed how things went when you followed a different path. It will be genuinely happy for you and support you whichever way you choose, as long as you are willing to learn from each and every experience.

Intuition can also help you forgive yourself, life, and others. If you tune in to a past event that causes you to hold grudges against yourself and others, you can quiet your conscious mind and calm your emotions, then ask for insights to help you understand what happened, as well as the people involved. This can help you to forgive and move on. (But please make sure this is not a traumatic event for which you may need professional help, such as a therapist.)

Kim was frustrated with her sister over a disagreement related to their family estate. She had been thinking about it for days, going around in circles in her mind. After she was able to calm and quiet her mind and emotions, I had her tune in to her sister. This included imagining her as a young girl. Kim could see that both she and her sister had grown up with insecurities about being in a family that favored boys. She realized that they had been competing for love and attention all their lives, and they could love and support each other instead.

Intuition Brings Compassion, and Vice Versa

Erik complained about an old classmate he had reconnected with in the last few years. "I think my gut told me that this guy was no good, not worth hanging out with anymore. He either cancels our plans with short notice or doesn't show up on time. His life is a mess. He reached out to me, so I guess he needs some kind of help. My intuition is saying that it's a waste of time to even try to help him out in any way. He will never follow through."

I paused as I took in Erik's words and the look of certainty on his face. "Are you sure that was your intuition talking and not just your conscious mind?" I was skeptical, since Erik's sentiments seemed very harsh.

As we dug in deeper, it turned out that Erik's intuition was mainly about his friend being in need of some support. The rest of the story and reactions were coming from Erik's conscious mind and high standards as a go-getter who did not have much patience with people he considered to be slow. Erik sheepishly said afterward, "I guess I was expecting him to be more like me, or the way he used to be when we were classmates in college."

As Erik came to understand, there is a beautiful link between compassion and intuition. Each feeds into the other, and each amplifies the presence of the other. Our intuition's clear insights will do their best to help us acknowledge the truth but not at the expense of degrading another person. As Erik discovered, it is often the conscious mind that rushes in to create stories in an attempt to help us to make sense of our insights—and to protect us. When we include our intuition in our interactions with others, it can lead to understanding them better, which can, in turn, evoke empathy and compassion. Because of their relaxing effect, practicing empathy and compassion for ourselves and others can also lead to more active intuition, as it primes our mind and emotions to move into a calmer state.

Intuition Precedes Our Conscious Thought Chain

I have designed an exercise for my students (which I will share in detail in chapter 7, but use to illustrate a point here), in which I show them pictures of people whom I know well, but my students have never met. I let them look at each picture for a few seconds, then ask them what character traits they're picking up about the person in the photograph.

Once, during this exercise, one of my students said, "This person really likes money and material things." I pointed out that this sounded more like a judgmental statement than intuition. I asked her if she had any prior thoughts that made her come to this conclusion. She thought for a few seconds before saying, "Yes, I thought that he probably could afford a nice car and a fancy house."

I told her to imagine pressing the delete key on a keyboard and erasing that thought. Then, I asked her if she'd had a previous thought leading to the one she'd just mentioned. She replied, "Yes, I thought he must have a good degree from a good university." Once again, I asked her to delete that thought. I kept asking her the same question as before: "What was the thought preceding this one?" We went on this way until she could not trace it back to any other thought. Her initial insight we came to was, "This person is smart, persistent, and hard-working."

"Bingo! That is completely accurate," I said. She was so blown away by this that we had to sit quietly for a while to let it sink in. This is the delete, delete, delete method I mentioned earlier. It allows you to retrace your insight back to its original intuitive form.

Training our intuition is a powerful way to help us clear existing prejudices we might not even realize we have. Using our intellect and intuition together in this way can make us more aware of our thoughts, some of which are biased judgments rather than accurate assessments of our experiences. Noticing them can help us push them aside. All positive change starts with awareness.

One thing to note is that retracing our thought patterns is not an unusual process; in fact, we do it quite frequently. For example, perhaps you start thinking about how to initiate a new part of a project for work. A few minutes later, you're wondering what to do with all the rusty paint cans in the garage, so you walk over to your garage. In your distracted state, you forget why you did so. But then you ponder for a moment and realize, "Oh, I know, I thought about how this phase of the project requires me to work with a different team, then I thought about working with that team on an older project. That old project made me think of the old things in the garage, and then about the rusty paint cans."

Sometimes, it can take a while to retrace our steps, but when we focus our attention and awareness, we realize that it's a lot easier than we may have believed.

Exercise: Expand Your Intuition Journal

I hope you've already begun to dig into the intuition journal exercise from chapter 1. If not, here is another chance to start—or expand that journal if you have already been using it. Your intuition journal is meant to familiarize you with how your intuition activates and under which conditions it flourishes.

Now, let's expand your journal entries to add any of the characteristics of intuition we've discussed in this chapter that you can identify in your intuitive encounters. You can do this for any new experiences, and you can also go back to your previous entries and add the characteristics there. You are basically expanding the database of your intuition to gain more clarity as to whether you're tapping in to your intuition or conscious thinking—such as a judgment that followed a chain of thoughts.

For example, if you meet someone and feel you don't want to become friends with them, and you wonder if your intuition is warning you, add this to your journal. Include the characteristics you noticed in that feeling. Did it have any preceding thoughts, conscious analysis, or judgments about the person, such as, "She looks so much like my old roommate, and I don't like my old roommate"? Did your conscious thinking go into scenario-writing mode under the influence of biases or prejudices? When you try to empty your mind of any of these, take a few deep breaths and reattune to your intuition, what information do you get? Does it seem to persist? Does it feel like a gentle nudge or a forceful fear? Observe and note whatever you are experiencing. Even if you conclude that it was your intuition speaking, be sure to consider the input of your conscious thinking and any other trusted sources in order to make your call.

Key Takeaways

- It's important to use both your intuition and your conscious mind, especially when you're about to make an important decision—but to be able to do this in a meaningful way, you need to be able to tell the difference between the two.

- Although you may not realize it, you are constantly putting your intuition to use. In fact, implicit learning, which occurs when your conscious mind isn't involved, is often a key part of your intuition. There are many daily functions we engage in on autopilot—and we often modify them intuitively, in the moment.

- Intuition doesn't generally knock us over the head with fearful or forceful thoughts and ideas; it is typically gentle. Our conscious mind might take over and write scary stories.

- Intuition can make even mundane tasks feel fun, like you're being taken on a grand adventure.

- Intuition often reinforces what you already know to be true.

- Intuition gives its message directly, and that message is typically the first thing that pops into our thoughts and sensations.

- At the same time, there is an art to interpreting intuition, as we might not always understand what we are receiving—in which case, it's always good to give ourselves time and to consult with our conscious mind and other sources.

- If what you got the first time was from your intuition, it will typically give the same answer when you ask again after calming your conscious mind and emotions.
- While our conscious mind tends to label people and situations as good or bad, our intuition is nonjudgmental.
- Accessing intuition isn't about getting the right outcome. Intuition teaches us that life is a continuous learning experience, and as long as we recognize this, we don't have to keep beating ourselves up over perceived mistakes. We can always begin again, exactly where we are.
- Intuition increases our sense of compassion toward ourselves and others; at the same time, exercising greater compassion enables us to tap into our intuition even more.
- Intuition helps us recognize our biases and prejudices and retrace our thoughts back to our original intuitive awareness.

Reflections

- Were there any characteristics of intuition that surprised you or that you disagree with? If so, reflect on your reasons—and on what you might add or change.
- What is something that you can now do because of implicit learning—that is, it has become embedded in your everyday life, and you don't have to consciously think about it to do it? Now, pretend you are teaching this to someone who doesn't know how to do it. What

happens when you attempt to consciously think about and explain this activity? Is it easy or difficult? What other thoughts and feelings arise?

- When have you mistaken your judgment for intuition? This week, watch for any times you have an initial hunch, and your mind starts writing a story about it. Try deleting the thought chain, as you learned in this chapter. When you do that, observe what happens. How does it change your connection to your intuition?

- How has your intuition helped you hone the forgiving, compassionate aspect of who you are? How might this help you in areas of your life where you may be struggling?

- How is your understanding of your intuition evolving now that you've learned about its primary characteristics?

CHAPTER 3

Calm Yourself to Hear Your Inner Wisdom— Priming for Intuition

The first step in learning to notice and improve intuition is to start building your own intuition database by noting when, how, and under which conditions it gets activated. After using your intuition journal for a few weeks, you'll start to notice patterns in the data you've collected. You may recognize, as most of my students and clients do, that your intuition becomes more active when you have ample quiet time, take better care of yourself, incorporate healthy habits and self-care routines, and experience calmer and more positive emotions.

To train our intuition to respond when we need to tap into it, we can learn from these recorded experiences. We can re-create the environment and the mental and emotional state our intuition thrives in as closely as possible. I refer to this kind of physical, mental, and emotional preparation for using our intuition as priming.

Most of the work I do with my students and clients is about exploring different ways of priming them for intuition, then openly observing whatever comes up. When I start to teach new students, I spend time getting to know them better so that I understand what makes them feel calm and happy.

This helps prime their intuition in ways that work well for them.

Our conscious thinking can take space and attention away from the subtle calls of our intuition. Priming helps to mitigate this by quieting our conscious thoughts and calming our emotional state. Priming allows us to practice getting out of our own way, which is wonderful for enabling our intuition to come forward and for experiencing greater peace in general.

Here, I want to emphasize that we all have various parts and voices that populate our inner dialogue. These include our self-sabotaging inner critic and various other characters that preside over our random chatter. We can treat these parts with compassion, as they first arose within us as coping mechanisms for dealing with our life circumstances. In fact, many of these voices have a positive root, as they come from our strengths, but life can unintentionally train us to misuse or overuse them. For example, over time, our leadership skills can give birth to a tendency to want to control everything and everyone around us. Priming helps us quiet those voices rather than engage with them. Of course, if you wish to understand these voices, there are forms of therapy and coaching that will help with that, which in turn will improve your connection to your intuition. For our purpose here, we won't be engaging with these voices at all; rather, we'll practice priming so that we can touch the source of our deep inner wisdom.

Intuition: A Game That Relaxes Us

Priming can alleviate many of the stressors that result in negativity and bad moods. Many scientific studies reveal that our intuition is more active and accurate when we are in a good mood, and it's less active and accurate if we are experiencing negative emotions. We have all experienced the way our attention becomes rigid and narrow when we are in a foul mood, and in contrast, how novel solutions and creative ideas arise when we're receptive and positive. This is intuition in action.

In their study that was published in Psychological Science in 2003, researchers Annette Bolte, Thomas Goschke, and Julius Kuhl tested how intuition worked when their test subjects were primed differently. In their paper, "Emotion and Intuition: Effects of Positive and Negative Mood on Implicit Judgments of Semantic Coherence," they defined intuition as the ability to come to better-than-average conclusions via the unconscious processing of information.

The research team showed that participants were able to intuitively find subtle associations between word groups that were weakly linked when they were primed to be in a positive mood beforehand. The study also showed that putting participants in a negative mood had the reverse effect, and their ability to find coherent links within the weakly linked word groups dropped significantly. This supports that a great way to prime ourselves for intuition is to get ourselves into the best possible mood. In another study, researchers Carina Remmers and Johannes Michalak revealed that when people experience intense negative emotions—the kind that might be experienced at the extreme of clinical depression—intuition is markedly impaired.

Relaxation is an important factor in a good mood. When we're relaxed, our mind is capable of switching from conscious thinking to intuition. In a 1985 study of ten-year-old children, Stephen J. Ceci and Urie Bronfenbrenner, psychologists at Cornell University, had participants sit in front of computer screens where geometric shapes periodically appeared. These shapes would suddenly jump to a different location on the screen. The kids were told to predict where the shapes were going to jump. There was a hidden pattern involving the type and color of the shape that was too complicated for the kids to consciously figure out. Initially, they were told that this was part of their schoolwork. After 750 trials, the researchers found that the children had not learned the pattern intuitively by observing where the shapes jumped. On the other hand, when they were told that they would get to play a game, they performed better. In the version of the study when they were told it was a game, they caught animals that darted across the screen with a net.

The animal images followed the same pattern as the geometric shapes in the previous experiment. When the task was a game, the kids relaxed and learned the pattern. They were able to predict where the images would jump. It seemed that when the kids relaxed and took it as a game instead of schoolwork, they were better able to engage their intuition and catch the pattern (and therefore the animals on the screen) unconsciously. As we relax and get into a playful state of mind in which we are not overthinking or analyzing a situation, our intuition can come forward. These are good reminders to begin thinking of our intuition as a fun game that we are all capable of playing.

The Mirror Lake of the Mind

Intuition pulls out information from our subconscious and unconscious. One way to create space for this nonconscious process is to step out of its way and allow our brains to allocate more power to intuition. We can achieve this by any method that helps us quiet down the chatter of our conscious thoughts and relax our emotional state—which is what priming allows us to do.

When you are working on cultivating your intuition, prior to it becoming second nature, priming yourself for it is very important. I demonstrate this to my students early in our lessons. First, I tell them to think of a question or situation they would like to get some intuitive input on. Then, I give them a few moments to tune in to their intuition, pay full attention, and see what it is relayed. They usually hesitate and start expressing thoughts and ideas that are clearly emerging from a conscious chain of thought. Even their words reveal this, as their sentences start with, "I think." Next, we go through a priming exercise: perhaps a guided meditation, mindful breathing, or listening to a piece of music they enjoy and can lose themselves in. The intuition they receive afterward is very different. It comes with clarity, and when they express it, their words typically start with, "I feel."

Priming for intuition elevates the mood and stills the mind, so your inner wisdom can easily come forward with its advice. Fortunately, there are ways to make it easy for your inner wisdom to speak up in its own way. As you can imagine, the way this is achieved varies for each person. For some people, meditation works, whereas for others, playing a computer game mindlessly does the trick.

Priming for intuition brings up the image of a pristine lake surface in my mind. Imagine a clean, beautiful lake in a quiet place in nature, surrounded by trees. The lake is so calm that its surface is like a mirror, reflecting the trees and the sky. Now, imagine taking a pebble and throwing it into the lake, and watching the ripples change the reflection on the surface.

When we prime ourselves for intuition, we are trying to get our mind and emotional state into that pristine, mirror-like calmness. The question we ask our intuition is just like the pebble that generates the ripples, which we can observe if we're in the mental and emotional state to pay attention.

Methods for Priming Your Intuition

Once you become accustomed to tapping into your intuition on demand, you'll find there are many shortcuts to stillness and relaxation, which we'll discuss a bit later in this chapter. Until then, here are some ways to prime yourself, which will also work well for those of you who have already been practicing with your intuition for a long time:

- Meditate in whichever tradition works best for you. Meditation is a great way to awaken our intuition and our awareness of it. When we meditate, we learn to quiet our minds and also be in the compassionate, loving, clear, calm state that allows us to be more open to receiving intuitive messages. Meditation can be as simple as closing your eyes, or even keeping them open and softening the gaze, while focusing on the breath without trying to change it. Start to meditate for a few minutes daily and gradually increase the duration. Each time you notice conscious thinking grabbing your attention, let these thoughts go without judgment, and return your attention to your breathing. Imagining the thoughts that appear in your mind as clouds that float away or balloons that drift off into the sky can help in releasing them.

- Practice empathy by thinking of something or someone you love. Empathy puts us in a calm state of mind that opens up our heart space, which is deeply connected to intuition. My student Moira enjoys imagining that she is cuddling her beloved dog, which helps her get into this state.

- Listen to music that relaxes you and makes you forget about your to-do lists and problems. Zooming in and focusing on one instrument or set of instruments, such as the piano or the strings, can help you go even deeper and keep conscious thoughts away. I love percussion instruments, and listening to them within a piece of music primes me really well, as the rhythm carries all my conscious thoughts away.

- Engage in some activity that puts you into a flow state: Play your musical instrument, do some coloring, paint, draw, bake, or do anything that you can lose yourself in. Psychologist Mihaly Csikszentmihalyi described the flow state as one in which we are so connected to an activity that we lose track of time and even a sense of who we are; we become one with the activity and go with its flow. Athletes, musicians, and artists often describe this as the state they are in when they create their best work. My student Mike is a medical researcher who loves making cups and bowls on the pottery wheel. He says he often gets his best research ideas during the moments when he feels like he is one with the clay.

- Find something beautiful or interesting and focus on one sensation at a time, such as looking at a beautiful flower to see every detail, without consciously thinking about it or analyzing it. Or perhaps you touch the petals of the flower and only focus on the sensations.[2]

- Go for a walk in nature; the quieter the place, the better—unless you thrive and relax more when you're around loved ones or other people in general. You can go out into nature, to a place that calls to you—perhaps a forest, hilltop or mountain, beach, lake, river, or any place where you can be safe and feel internally calm and quiet.

- Create your own sanctuary and visit it often. You might find a spot in your home where you feel calm and at peace. For some people, this may be their office when no one else is there, or the garage or backyard. Consider putting up a one-person tent in your backyard or in the corner of a room, where you can find refuge from the hustle and bustle of your day. Kids are great at finding or creating their own sanctuaries, putting a blanket over the back of a sofa to play underneath it or setting up a spot for themselves under the dining table. Be inspired

---

[2] Shirzad Chamine's *Positive Intelligence* book and program call these brief focused attention meditation and mindfulness practices Positivity Quotient (PQ) reps.

by the little ones and carve out a place for yourself.

- If you don't have access to a quiet place, walk around in your environment and practice mindfulness of the sounds you hear. Just pay attention to the sounds without judging or thinking about them. The moment you notice that you're trying to figure out the source of a sound, or what makes it so loud, or any other conscious thought, just let it go and gently return your attention to only listening to the sounds, as if they were music. Work with what you have instead of resisting it.

- Visit a vista point, seaside, or any other place with a beautiful view, and just gaze out on the horizon, letting it relax you and melt your thoughts away. If there is no pleasant place nearby or one that's easily accessible, look at a picture of such a place or imagine being there, while taking deep breaths.

- Think of a time when you felt calm, serene, and happy. Imagine it as vividly as possible so you can relive it in your mind. My client Gloria usually imagined going back to her grandparents' cozy home, where she felt safe and filled with joy.

- Play with kids or pets—or watch them play. Children especially are so adept at dancing around, being silly, releasing their inner joy, and accessing their intuition in every moment. We can learn a thing or two from them.

- Let yourself engage in a fun and silly game, like you did when you were a child. Jeff, one of my clients who loves to be creative, once made silly hats out of whatever was around, which allowed him to get into a playful state and release his worries.

When you practice these priming methods or any that you come up with, over time you can begin to quiet your thoughts by simply imagining doing any of these activities. This can be just like pressing the mute button inside your head.

Priming yourself for intuition with the aforementioned activities is like using training wheels on a bicycle. You can drop them once you get a good sense of the state you are able to create in your mind and emotions that open up your intuition. You can call on that stillness on demand and be able to access your intuition easily once you get comfortable with practice over time.

Once your thoughts quiet down and your emotions settle into a calm, content state with priming, you can then ask your inner wisdom the question you want intuitive guidance on. In that stillness and openness, you will get an answer. Remember that silence can be an answer too. It may be telling you that this is not the right time to receive a specific answer to your question. You can thank your inner wisdom for the answer you receive, even if it was silence, and run this message through the filter of your logic and conscious mind. Then, you can add this inner advice to all the factors and inputs you will consider.

When I studied with my teachers, I usually learned to access my intuition through meditative states. This is not because intuition can only be accessed in that way. It was mainly due to my teachers' learning and teaching styles. Also, they had observed that their students responded well to this kind of teaching. That was why I was drawn to these teachers, to begin with.

I currently have a student, Alex, who is a data scientist. From the beginning, he told me he did not respond well to meditation. So, just like I do with all my students, we started by exploring what made his mind and emotions calm and receptive. In our first session, we went through his memories of when he could access intuitive messages; how he received them; and in what kinds of places, times, and settings. As we figured out more of the conditions that enabled his intuition to become active, the next step was to find a way to emulate those conditions to help Alex access his intuition on demand. This involved Alex mentally recalling specific times when he was more in touch with those qualities and he sensed his intuition being active. We had him practice this many times as we continued to explore and note every time he caught himself having an intuitive idea. I asked Alex to record these incidents in detail. We reviewed them to see if we could recreate those conditions, even if only in his imagination, to prime his intuition. While we built up and fine-tuned his practice this way, he was also acquiring valuable experience in accessing his intuition on demand.

Again, there are many ways of accessing your intuition. You are already using some of these in your daily life, whether you notice it or not. As we go through the different tools and lessons in this book, the goal is to enrich and increase your many ways of accessing your intuition. This is so you can have many options to choose from in a variety of situations.

Create Your Own Intuition Gesture

A great habit to build, which I teach all my students, is creating and routinely using an *intuition gesture* that can be repeated every time you want to work with your intuition.

This is a very important step that wires the brain to connect the intuition gesture to the primed state. It works as a shortcut to priming yourself for intuition when you don't have much time or you're with other people. After some weeks of practicing tapping into your intuition, including preparing yourself by using one of the priming methods and going into your intuition gesture when you feel primed and ready, you can start using the intuition gesture by itself. This will help you access your intuition more quickly and easily. It creates classical conditioning, also referred to as Pavlovian conditioning, after Ivan Pavlov, a physiologist of the nineteenth century.

Many of my students and clients choose the very universal gesture of putting their dominant hand on their heart. Some of them prefer to put their hand on the belly or gut instead, as they associate this center with their inner wisdom. A few of my students like to put their palms together in front of their chest in prayer pose. Some choose a more subtle gesture, such as putting the tips of the thumb and the index or middle finger together, creating a mudra of intention.

You can pick one of these or you can create your own intuition gesture that fits you and your life best. As you start to practice calling on your intuition, remember to include your intuition gesture just as you're about to drop your question into the stillness of your primed state.

Simplify Your Question

The act of asking your intuition a specific question is very important in the process of accesing it on demand. Prime your intuition right before dropping your question into your newly acquired calm, relaxed state.

Sometimes, you will have many possible paths you can take or choices you can make. If it feels difficult to get a clear intuitive message on which one to choose, try narrowing your choices by going through each of them and asking if that choice is the right one. It is very quick and easy to get yes or no answers to simplified questions. You can also experiment with this before you analyze and compare your choices with your intellect and logic. After priming yourself, then connecting to your intuition gesture, you can ask your intuition if the first choice is a yes or a no, then move on to the next choice, and so on. For any of the choices, if you hesitate and feel that the answer was not clear, you can take a few deep breaths, use a shorter version of priming (such as imagining yourself in a beautiful and relaxing place), connect to your intuition gesture, and ask again.

When our intuition knows that a given choice is not right for us, we repeatedly get no as the answer to this choice. You can also say this out loud and check how you feel when you say it. If it feels and rings true when you say, "This choice is not right for me," then your intuition is most likely pretty sure about not opting for that specific choice.

Let's run through this method using an example. Suppose you are in the market to buy a new car, and you have narrowed down your choices through your research and are considering three different cars. For simplicity, let's call them the *fancy* one, which will stretch your budget but feel wonderful to drive; the *mediocre* one, which will fit your needs and your budget perfectly and feel fine to drive; and the *basic* one, which will take care of your critical needs and leave some excess funds to spend on other necessities or small indulgences.

To tap into your intuition by simplifying the "Which car is the best fit for me?" question, you can go through each option and ask, "Is this the right car for me?" Do this only after you have primed yourself and connected to your intuition gesture.

Of course, there will be times when our questions aren't simple yes or no ones, and we are striving to receive as much insight or information as possible. I once had a client, May, who was starting a new social organization for parents of young children in the school district where she taught. She was eager to make the organization grow quickly, so she asked her intuition, "How do I get more parents to join my organization?" I gently told her, "This is the kind of question that might be better suited for your thinking mind—or even a marketing consultant."

Often, questions that are trying to elicit a particular outcome (more people, more clients, more money, more love) are not ideal for your intuition. It's good to pare down your questions into bite-size ones that help you gain greater clarity or know which next step is the right one to take. However, your intuition is not the best resource to turn to if you want an elaborate plan for how to get something you want. It is ideal for questions that help us in our learning and growth journeys, and that enable us to expand our hearts and connect with ourselves and others more deeply.

I recommended that May hone her questions further. We brainstormed on some possibilities, such as: "What's something I'm missing or not seeing here?" "What's the best next step for me?"

May decided to go with "What's the best next step for

me?" She got that it would be a good idea to start considering the types of parents who would most benefit from her offering. This inspired her to sit down and think about the specific issues her organization would help with. She quickly realized that the parents who seemed to need the most support were the ones whose children were struggling due to special needs and learning differences. She recognized that she needed to work on her organization's goals and manifesto a little bit more before she officially launched. Her capacity to rework her questions for her intuition helped her see that she wasn't ready and required more time to ensure her offering would be of benefit to her target audience.

In general, it's a great idea to learn how to frame your questions, because an ineffective question, when posed to your intuition, can generate confusion. Too often, this can make people feel like their intuition isn't working, but it can be as simple as changing the focus and wording of your question.

Overall, ineffective questions tend to be too large and general. They're also overly focused on outcomes for a desired future. Ineffective questions also tend to ask for a detailed, step-by-step set of instructions from beginning to end, which is not something that intuition responds to well—especially because there are all kinds of variables in your life and environment that could cause things to shift. In addition, ineffective questions are often focused on changing someone else's behavior. They might include: "How can I make my spouse do their fair share of the household chores?" "How do I get my mother to stop being so negative and passive-aggressive?" "How can I make my boss more appreciative of my efforts?"

Now, let's look at the characteristics of effective questions.

Because intuition is well purposed for helping you identify first steps and on offering you information that supports your personal growth, it's better to leave the door open to solutions and ideas you might not have previously considered. Effective questions, as I mentioned earlier, tend to sound like: What's missing here? What am I not seeing? What am I resisting? What is the best first step I can take, with what I know right now? Also, remember that intuition is not about controlling someone else's behavior, but about focusing on how you can change your own perspective or outlook, or find areas for your own personal growth. If you're having issues with your spouse, mother, or boss, you might ask a question like: How can I create more harmony in this relationship, to the best of my ability? What can I do to stand up for myself?

When I don't have any specific questions for my intuition but would still like to communicate with it and practice, I ask, "What is something healing that I can do for myself today?" You can also prepare your questions in advance; note them on a piece of paper or the notes app on your phone to pull them out when you are primed.

Exercise: Six Steps to Tap into Intuition

Often, my one-on-one lessons and my classes will shift based on my intuition in the moment about what my students need, want, or feel. But even when I go with the flow, I still include structured, step-by-step instructions for people who learn better that way. In general, I try to capture my students' different learning styles in our early sessions. For some, a step-by-step approach with specific goals helps, whereas for others, a free flow and experimentation inspire them.

If you benefit from step-by-step instructions, which can be especially helpful for beginners, here is the basic formula for tapping into your intuition. Keep these in mind and jot down notes in your journal with respect to how you experience each step.

Step 1. Priming: Still the mind and elevate the mood.

You can use any of the methods discussed in this chapter. I think of this step as letting go of negative emotions by relaxing the body and soul and calming down the mind to create a blank page, clean slate, or mirrorlike surface. Once you achieve this state through your priming method, bask in it for a few moments before you go to the next step.

Step 2. Use your intuition gesture.

Put your hand on your heart or belly, bring the tips of your thumb and index and middle finger together, touch your chin, or do anything that you feel comfortable repeating anywhere, anytime when you need to connect with this primed state of still mind and elevated mood.

Step 3. Drop your question into the stillness.

In your mind, or if it is comfortable, out loud, ask the question you want intuitive guidance on. You can imagine dropping the question on a blank page or the surface of a beautiful calm lake, if you like visualizing. While doing this, stay connected to your primed state. If you notice you are starting to think and consciously analyze the question, imagine pressing a reset button and return to your priming method for a few minutes.

Then, drop your question into the stillness once you feel ready.

Step 4. Pay attention in full alertness to receive an answer.
Wait for an answer, which can come as a knowing or a sensation. Make sure you are not consciously thinking about the question or analyzing the situation before coming to a conclusion. If you are, then the answer would come from your logical conscious analysis. In that case, go back to your priming method to relax and quiet your thoughts. Then, drop your question into the stillness of your mind again. If you are not sure what your intuition is saying, do another round of quick priming and ask again, or ask a follow-up question to clarify the message you are receiving.

Step 5. Run the answer through the filter of conscious reasoning.
When you get an answer from your intuition that is not the result of a conscious thought chain, compare what it says to what your logic and intellect advise. It is always a good idea to see if your intuition holds up when you think about its answer. Intuition and intellect are complements, not competitors. It is best to use both before making important decisions.

Step 6. Evaluate all factors altogether, including intuition.
Add your intuition to the set of all other inputs you will consider to make a decision before you take an action. Remember that your intuition is one of many factors, not the only factor you will need to take into account in most situations. You need to put all your cards on the table and weigh each factor to make the best possible decision.

Let's run through these steps with the example of buying a car. As mentioned earlier, you've already done the research required to narrow down your choices and make sure they are viable. Once you've done this homework, you can create the best environment possible to tap into your intuition about your final decision. You can do a simple meditation, such as following your breath for a few minutes, or you can choose a different priming method that works for you, such as lying on the grass and gazing at the sky until your thoughts quiet down. Remember to bring in your intuition gesture. Then, you can drop the question, "Which car is the best fit for me?", into the stillness of your mind. You can close your eyes and wait for any images or ideas to pop into your mind as your intuition speaks up about this choice. Maybe you see yourself driving down a scenic highway in your dream car, or you just know that the sensible budget car is the choice you will not have any regrets about. Once your intuition speaks up in its own way, run this answer through the filter of your conscious analytical mind and see if it holds up. Then, you can include what your intuition says along with all other factors—such as your research results, family and friends' advice, and your logical conclusions—in your final decision.

Key Takeaways

- *Priming* is physical, mental, and emotional preparation for using our intuition.
- Priming can help relax us and put us in a good mood, and scientific studies reveal that our intuition is more

active and accurate when we are relaxed and feeling positive emotions.

- Priming for intuition stills the mind, creating the kind of mirrorlike surface you might find on a still lake, so your inner wisdom can easily come forward with its advice through "ripples."

- There are various methods for priming your intuition, ranging from meditation (such as focusing on your breath), to practicing empathy, to allowing yourself to let loose and be playful. Choose the methods that work best for you.

- Creating an intuition gesture works as a shortcut to priming yourself for intuition when you don't have much time or you're with other people.

- Simplifying the question that you drop into your intuition, as well as learning to ask effective questions, can help you to access your intuition more easily and readily.

Reflections

- What metaphor works best for you when you think of or sense into a calm, relaxed state of mind? Perhaps it's the mirrorlike surface of a lake, or a cloudless sky.

- What kinds of activities help you relax, put you in an elevated mood, and quiet down your conscious thoughts? Do they coincide with the priming techniques in this chapter? How can you customize these activities for priming your intuition?

- What is an intuition gesture you can easily use each time you practice priming yourself and add to your intuition toolkit as a shortcut for priming later on?
- Create a list of questions that you'd like to ask your intuition. Using the information in this chapter regarding effective versus ineffective questions, consider whether it might be a good idea to reframe any of your questions.

CHAPTER 4

Expand Your Palate—More Practices to Prime
for Intuition

Tapping into intuition on demand is a skill that improves with practice. Scientific studies, such as the 2016 one conducted by researchers Galang Lufityanto, Chris Donkin, and Joel Pearson, support this.

When practicing intuition, you need to remember that the goal is not about attaining a specific level of accuracy. It's a good idea to let go of excess enthusiasm when you get things right and of disappointment when you get things wrong. First of all, right and wrong are usually highly subjective concepts. What seems wrong may be right at other levels or from other angles, and vice versa. We are also all very familiar with the concept of the timing being wrong, even if the actual situation seems right.

The key to practicing intuition is being open to possibilities and having a childlike, curious, playful attitude. As you practice tapping into your intuition, you also learn about yourself and gain deep insights. You get a sense of what kinds of things or people you connect with more easily and how you receive messages from your intuition. There is no end to what you can learn from your intuition. One of the best ways to explore is by experimenting and gaining experience through daily practice. This chapter will pick up on where we left off in chapter 3, as you'll learn step-by-step priming techniques for tapping into your intuition.

As I mentioned before, these are not the only ways to prime yourself. I have observed them work well with most of my students and clients, but you may be inspired to try other things. They are included here in detail to give you ideas and general guidance on how to create your own priming meditations and methods.

From here on out, we'll be delving into a lot of experiential exercises to help you expand your familiarity with your intuition. As a reminder, throughout these exercises, I will frequently guide you to imagine a place, person, or situation. The purpose is to give your mind something to focus on to stop the conscious thinking process and relax your emotions and mood as much as possible.

You don't need to believe that what you are imagining or visualizing is actually true. You don't even need to see it vividly in your mind. All you need to do is keep an open and playful attitude as you move through the exercises that involve imagining scenes or situations. If you are not a visual person, you can focus more on your other senses as you imagine these scenes into being. They are mainly aimed at quieting the mental chatter and letting go of stress and worries for the moment so that your intuition can come forward and make itself known. Some of the exercises where we use metaphors (which we'll explore further in chapter 6) or objects will also help your intuition speak and enable your conscious thinking to get out of the way.

Sacred Space Meditation for Priming

The following exercise is meant to quiet your mind so that your intuition can communicate with you and be heard more clearly.[3] We will be journeying into a very refreshing and safe place. In the beginning of all priming meditations, we will put our attention on anchoring sensations, such as the breath, to relax our minds and to gently brush away our thoughts. If you feel uncomfortable at any point during any of these exercises, just bring your attention back to your breath, observe it going in and out for a few cycles, then bring your awareness to your physical surroundings. Take your time and when it is comfortable to do so, gently open your eyes by fluttering them to get used to your environment. If you are not a visual person and other senses are more dominant for you, feel free to modify the following guidance to focus more on those other senses. For example, instead of visualizing colors, imagine feeling the temperature or texture of a detail that is described visually.

1. Think of a question you would like intuitive guidance on. This can be anything you might ask a good friend, such as:
   a. What is the next step I need to take in my job search?
   b. How can I connect better with my teenage son?
   c. Where can we go this weekend to feel rejuvenated?

---

[3] Audio recordings of the guided meditation exercises can be found at nildemircubuk.com.

2. Write this question on a piece of paper, fold it up, and put it in your pocket—or simply imagine doing so. You can also write it down in your intuition journal.

3. Sit or lie down in a comfortable place and position. Close your eyes if it feels fine. If not, you can soften your gaze or partially close your eyes.

4. Put your attention on your breathing. Follow each breath as it goes in through your nose, down your windpipe, and into your lungs. Observe how your chest and belly expand on each in-breath. As you breathe out, notice your chest or belly move and the air going out through your nose. There is no need to try to change your breathing, but it can naturally deepen or feel different just because you are paying attention to it, which is completely normal. You can add a color to your breath if that makes it easier to follow it. It can be a mist in a beautiful, soothing hue.

5. Now imagine a source of white and gold light a few feet above your head. This source of light is like a showerhead that rains white light with gold shimmers. Pick different colors if they are more soothing for you. This light runs over and around your body and also through your body. It washes away all tension, pain, discomfort, fear, anxiety, worries, and anything else you don't want to hold on to and that does not serve you. You can imagine these coming out from your fingertips and the bottoms of your feet as gray smoke or a liquid that runs down, over, and through your body and disappears into the ground. With each in-breath, imagine more and more of this cleansing

light coming over and through you and bringing you a sense of peace; with each out-breath, feel all the negativity evaporating.

6. As you start to feel relaxed, imagine this shower of light expanding out and starting to reveal a beautiful place. This is your sacred space. It may be a place that you have been to before or you may create it from scratch right now. It can also be a new version of a favorite space that you can modify to make even more comfortable. Wherever it is, this place is yours alone, and you can come back whenever you want. Here, you can experience your authentic self with no judgment, no goals, and no interference from others.

7. Look around and explore your sacred space. Awaken all your senses and go through them one by one. Fill the space with shapes and colors. Walk around and touch surfaces, bringing all your attention to this tactile sensation. Listen to all the sounds and take in all the smells you can. Even if you've been here before, you can still explore with a beginner's mind and let yourself notice anything new.

8. When you feel that you have explored this place fully, pick your favorite spot. You might choose to lie down on the sand or grass or sit on a comfortable chair or sofa with a breathtaking view. Take a few moments to sink in.

9. When you feel ready, bring in your intuition gesture, such as putting your hand over your heart or belly. Do this physically in your meditation chair or where you are lying down.

10. Once you are connected to this gesture in your physical environment and in your imagined sacred space, drop the question that you prepared for your intuition into the stillness of this place. Add some more playfulness here to go even deeper into priming if you like. If there is water, you may imagine writing this question down on a piece of paper and releasing it into the water, or copying your question on a pebble and dropping it in. If the ground is sand or soil, you might picture writing your question on that surface. If there is a beautiful bird or butterfly, perhaps you whisper to it. For some people, this space may be technologically advanced and have extremely powerful computers and other research tools they trust. They might choose to type their question on a keyboard or drop it into a beaker on a lab table. Be playful and open and create your own way to drop your question into this sacred place.

11. Now, take another deep, cleansing breath, and as you exhale, let any remaining tension melt away. Lean back if you are sitting, sink into the ground or floor if you are lying down, and wait for the answer to your question to come. It may come on the wings of a bird or in a bottle from the waves on the water. It may appear as writing in the sand or soil or in the sky as a line of clouds. It can show up on a screen. Be open and willing to receive an answer. If the answer comes inside something you need to open or unfold, do so in a playful way, perhaps by covering what contains the message in pure white and gold light.

12. If nothing comes, take a few more deep breaths and look around; pay attention to what you feel and wait. If still no answer comes, thank everything in your sacred space and yourself for trying, and consider the possibility that this may not be the right time for you to have a clear answer. Everything required for an answer to exist may still be in motion and evolving.

13. If you receive an answer, thank your sacred space and your messengers, and take the message with you in whatever way you like. If the message was written on a piece of paper, imagine putting it in your pocket, or holding it over your heart for a few moments to absorb it.

14. Whether you received a message or not, recognizing that the absence of an answer can also be a message, thank this beautiful, sacred space and everything in it for your experience.

15. Take a few deep, cleansing breaths again, bringing your attention more and more to the sensations around your breath each time. Follow your breath for a few cycles.

16. Next, slowly start to bring your attention to where you are sitting or lying down in your current physical environment. Feel the seat, the chair, the bed, or the floor. Take a few moments to rest, knowing where you are physically.

17. When you feel ready, slowly flutter open your eyes, maybe blinking a few times. When your eyes are fully open, look around and observe where you are.

18. Then, think of the answer or message you received in

your sacred space. If you have a way to record it, feel free to do so. If you have the time, sit or lie down with this message for a few moments before you get up and go on with the rest of your day.

Now that you have created your sacred space, you can practice this exercise in a shorter time when you would like to revisit the space and ask for intuitive guidance in the stillness. Stay open to the possibility of your sacred space evolving or changing over time. There's no need to get attached to it being a specific way and exactly the same upon each visit. You can also create multiple sacred spaces that you can choose from depending on your mood. Each time you create a new sacred space, fill it with as much detail as possible. Remember to take general notes about your sacred spaces in your journal, especially if you are aiming to have multiple places to choose from each time you want to repeat this exercise.

I tell my students and clients that they don't have to tell me about their sacred space if they want to keep it to themselves. Still, some of them share enthusiastically after I guide them through this meditation. Mahir had many options in the beginning of the meditation, as he was a world traveler, but he picked the old stone schoolhouse in his idyllic hometown that he used to visit frequently during his childhood. He especially loved a corner in the backyard under his favorite tree, which became his favorite spot in his sacred space. Another client, Joanna, was dreaming about opening a yoga studio, so she built it in her imagination to use it as her sacred space. I personally like to go to a quiet, secluded beach that is a modified collage of beaches I have seen. Whatever you choose, make it yours and imagine being there with all your senses to go deeper into the zone of your relaxed, quiet mind and emotions.

Once you have created your sacred space or multiple sacred spaces, you can revisit these quickly while at work, in the store, or with other people around. Here is a modified, shorter version of the meditation.

1. Start by softening your gaze or looking at a distant point, the way you would if you were in deep thought.
2. Take a deep, cleansing, light-filled breath and exhale slowly, letting tensions wash away.
3. Go to your sacred space in your mind, imagining it as vividly as you can for a moment or two.
4. Drop your question into the stillness in your preferred way and wait for an answer to come.
5. If you don't receive an answer, take another deep, cleansing breath, and give it another moment.
6. Thank your sacred space and the universe for the answer you receive, or the lack of an answer, which may also be a message in itself.
7. Look around to reorient yourself to where you are physically.
8. If possible, record the message that you received in your journal.

Flow Activity

For this exercise, pick an activity that puts you in a flow state, which we discussed in chapter 3. This can be any activity that causes you to lose track of time in a pleasurable way. For some of my students, this involves an art, such as playing a musical instrument or painting. For others, it can be a sport or a recreational activity, such as running or hiking. Some prefer computer games they can practically play on autopilot.

1. Before you get into your flow activity, think of a question or situation you would like intuitive guidance on. Open your calendar or favorite reminder app and set an alert with the question in the title of the calendar entry or reminder. Allocate enough time to get into your flow activity and to really lose yourself in it before the reminder pops up.

2. Start your flow activity and enjoy. Keep your phone or other device nearby, so you can see the alert when it comes up; however, avoid getting into your texts or social media. Just focus on your flow activity. Paint, walk, bake, and let go of time and to-do lists as you fully engage in what makes you feel happy and relaxed.

3. When the reminder alert sounds, connect to your intuition gesture.

4. Drop your question into your intuition. Wait for an answer to come to your awareness. Be open to receiving messages that are related to your flow activity, which may lead to more revelations later on. If you were painting, you might feel called to paint something different. If you were walking, you could be inspired to turn and continue in a new direction. As long as it is safe for you and others, try to follow the creative guidance and see what comes out of it.

5. If you receive an answer to your question, note it in your intuition journal.

My student Sofia loved to garden so much that she completely lost track of time when tending to her flowers and the vegetables she grew. This was the perfect practice ground for her to try this exercise. She wrote down, "What is the next step in my graduate-school applications?" for her intuition in her journal. She set it aside until she was done with her gardening then captured the first thing that popped up in her awareness when she looked at her question. Sofia had been procrastinating on her applications. She was inspired and motivated to complete them in the next few days, based on the guidance she received.

If your time is tight, or your environment doesn't lend itself to engaging in your favorite flow activity, you can imagine it instead. You can do this in a few minutes. After you practice a few times, you can learn to connect to the flow feeling quickly and easily. Here's an abbreviated version of the exercise:

1. Close your eyes if you can or soften your gaze and imagine yourself fully engaged in your flow activity. This also opens the door to trying hobbies you may not have had the time or opportunity to engage in for a long time. You can sail, hang-glide, climb a mountain peak, or anything else you'd like to do in your imagination. Choose anything you would thoroughly enjoy and can imagine doing as vividly as possible.

2. When you feel relaxed, content, and in the flow,

ask your question and wait for an answer from your intuition.

3. As in the full version of this exercise, be open to receiving the answer in various ways.

After Sofia used her flow activity of gardening to prime herself for intuition on several occasions, she was then able to just close her eyes and imagine gardening. She got into her imagination so much that she could almost feel and smell the rich soil in her hands.

Take Your Intuition for a Walk

When you feel stuck and that your intuition has been really quiet lately, take it out for a walk. It is best to do so in a relatively quiet area where you can be in nature and exposed to the fresh air. You can pick a low-traffic neighborhood close to where you live, a nearby park, or a forest—wherever you will be safe.

You can practice mindful walking by focusing your attention either on your feet or legs, experiencing every step fully. If that does not feel right or safe due to heavy traffic, you can keep your attention on your surroundings. Look around and notice beautiful things, such as birds, flowers, trees, the sky, the clouds, and intentionally let go of your thoughts.

If you can find a circular route that is not too small, such as a path around a park or alongside a river, you can try walking that loop. You can keep your attention on different parts of your body that are moving, focusing on each for a few cycles of breath. You can combine this with the intention of quieting down your conscious thinking and bring your attention back to your feet, legs, arms or other parts of your body when you notice conscious thoughts come up.

Once you feel primed, in a calm mental and emotional state, you can connect to your intuition gesture and ask your question. Pay close attention so that you can capture the first thing that pops up in your awareness, be it a word, symbol, sentence, or silence.

As always, thank your intuition for its input, even if all you received was silence.

Diamond Light Meditation

This is another meditative exercise to prime for intuition.

1. You can prepare a question you want to ask your intuition and write it on a piece of paper or in your intuition journal, then set it aside or imagine doing so.
2. Sit or lie down comfortably in a place where you will not be disturbed.
3. Start to observe your breath going in and out of your nostrils, down and then up your windpipe, into and out of your lungs. Notice how your chest and belly expand when you breathe in and how they contract when you breathe out. Keep following the breath gently without forcing it in any way. If you are not comfortable following your whole breath, you can focus on only part of it, such as your chest or abdomen moving gently. You can put one hand on your chest or abdomen to make this even easier and just pay attention to how

your hand gently moves as you breathe. Your breathing may naturally become deeper when you start paying attention to it. Just notice this without any attachment or judgment. If this feels difficult, try to imagine the breath as a mist in a beautiful color, going in and out of your body.

4. After a few more cycles of following the breath, move your attention to your core. This is the area in the center of your body.

5. Imagine a point between your abdomen and your back. Picture a tiny dot of silvery white light, like a pinhead. Imagine it growing to the size of a walnut or golf ball, with silvery white light coming out of its surface in every direction in extra-thin rays that are thinner than a strand of hair.

6. Imagine that the light coming out of this diamond source spreads to your whole body, reaching every part. This beautiful source is transmitting light into your body, just like your heart pumps life force into your veins, all the way to your fingers and toes and the top of your head. Bask in this beautiful light as it fills your body and imagine that it has a relaxing and healing effect.

7. If you feel tension, pain, or discomfort in any part of your body, you can imagine the silvery white light coming from your diamond light source resting in those areas a bit longer as the rays flow through and concentrate their soothing radiance. See or imagine this light, which is your own inner light. Linger on

points of tension, pain, or discomfort, and then let it continue to flow.

8. Allow the silvery white light from your diamond source to reach outside your body. Start to see your inner light expand outward and form a cocoon that reaches about one arm's length from your body. Bask in this soothing cocoon of light, seeing yourself sitting or lying down inside it. Feel how relaxing and empowering it is to sit inside this cocoon of your inner light. Enjoy it for a few moments.

9. Bring in your intuition gesture when you feel ready.

10. Now, you can drop the question you prepared for your intuition into this stillness of mind and emotions. Notice what comes up as a response, including words and symbols. Thank your intuition, even if all you get is silence.

11. You can also say the following affirmation or other comforting and encouraging words to yourself quietly or out loud: "I recognize my symbolic inner light and allow it to shine even beyond my physical presence. I continue my life being aware of this light within me. I am strong and ready to experience my own light and live fully."

12. You can now turn your attention back to your breath. As before, follow it going in and out of your nostrils, down and then up your windpipe, and into and out of your lungs. Give your breath a color if that makes it easier to follow. Stay with your breath for a few cycles.

13. When you feel ready, gently start to move your shoul-

ders, arms, and legs. Wiggle your fingers and toes. Feel where you are sitting or lying down. You can flutter your eyes open slowly and look around to reorient yourself to your environment.

14. Take a few minutes to write about this experience in your intuition journal before you move on with the rest of your day.

You can use the diamond light imagery as a quick way of priming after practicing the full version a few times. If you need to tap into your intuition and time is short or the environment doesn't lend itself to meditating, just imagine the walnut or golf ball–sized source of silvery white diamond light in the center of your body. Set the intention to quickly fill your whole body with this light and expand it out about an arm's length. Now, you can ask your intuition the question you have and notice what comes up.

A couple of my clients who are managers and need to attend many meetings love to use this quick version of the diamond light meditation at work. One of them says that it reminds her of the "ever present and quietly waiting" inner wisdom that can shine light onto the situation at hand. She even came up with the idea of wearing a bracelet that has a bead resembling a diamond so as not to forget to turn her inner diamond light on and tap into her intuition, in addition to using her logic.

Water Meditation

If you don't have a fear of water or trauma related to it, imagining yourself in clear, clean water can be a soothing way to calm your thoughts and emotions, helping to open the door to your intuition. Follow the guidance here if it feels comfortable for you.

1. Settle into a comfortable, quiet place where you won't be disturbed. Close your eyes or soften your gaze.
2. Imagine a gentle, colorful mist surrounding you, lifting you up. Let yourself float in space and time, arriving at a serene natural setting.
3. Feel a plush carpet of fresh grass beneath your feet. Smell the plants and trees around you and listen to the birds and leaves that rustle in the breeze.
4. Spot a beautiful pond of clear, inviting water ahead. Walk toward it, taking in the details—smooth stones, plants surrounding it, and clear water.
5. Walk into the water, which is the perfect temperature for you. You can stand with your head and shoulders above the water or submerge yourself completely.
6. Cup your hands and gather some water. As you lift your palms, notice the sunlight sparkling in the water.
7. With the intention of releasing all tension and quieting your mind, pour the water over your head. Repeat this as many times as you like, feeling your thoughts quieting with each pour.

8. Once you're deeply relaxed, ask your intuition a question. If nothing specific comes to mind, ask for a message to improve an area of your life.
9. For added fun, imagine a fish or duck arriving to receive your question and deliver the answer. Let your intuition speak through them.
10. Once you receive your answer—whether it's a clear message or silence—thank your intuition.
11. Step out of the water and return to your mist, which lifts you and takes you back to your physical environment. Feel the contact points of where you're sitting or lying.
12. Gently move your arms, hands, and fingers. Wiggle your toes. Slowly open your eyes.
13. Take a moment to reorient yourself and capture your experience. Journal your insights or record a voice memo to reflect on the messages received.

Empty Out

I took a voice-building class for actors a few years ago. We had several exercises that we went through to build a strong voice and toolkit to be able to sing. Some of the most important exercises involved expanding our lungs and strengthening our diaphragm.

At the beginning of each of these exercises, we would put our hands up in the air and quickly and forcefully bring them down to our sides, pushing the diaphragm and the lungs in, and exhaling all the breath we still had inside. Appropriately, our teacher called this the empty out method.

As we strengthen our intuition muscles, we also need to do the empty out part. In these exercises, we are emptying out our thoughts and our mental habits and any accompanying negative emotions. These include consciously evaluating matters to come to conclusions and judgments about them. So, if it helps—before you tune in to a question that you would like to receive an intuitive answer to—put your arms up and forcefully bring them down to your sides with an exhale. Say to yourself, "Empty out," with the intention of clearing your mind. You can also simply imagine yourself doing this. And if you are out with other people, you can do a subtle version of this with just your hands or fingers moving as you exhale.

Chest and Belly Wave Breathing

Many different breathing techniques can be used for priming yourself. One I like involves bringing your attention to your chest and belly rising and falling as you breathe in and out. When you start practicing this, you can put one hand on your chest and the other on your belly to make it easier to feel them moving.

1. Take a deep breath and feel your chest and belly move outward as you inhale and move inward as you exhale.
2. After a few cycles of this, notice if your chest moves more than your belly or the other way around. Let thoughts and judgments go—just breathe and focus all your attention on the movement.
3. In the next breath, set the intention of having your belly move more than your chest, then alternate in the

following breath, keeping all your attention on the movement and quieting your mind.

4. When your mind and emotions are relaxed, you can connect to your intuition gesture and ask your intuition any question you have, since you are nicely primed. As always, weigh your intuition against what your logic says on that topic before you make your final decision or take an action.

Give Your Intuition a Persona

It may be easier for you to communicate with your inner wisdom as if it is a wise person you can go to for advice. You can give your intuition a name or persona. Then, tune in to your intuition for a question you have. You can also do a simple daily intuition check-in, during which you have a dialogue with this character that is actually part of yourself.

Just remember that your intuition is still an integral part of you and not something outside of yourself, even if you give it a persona for easier communication. One of my students, Katie, liked to imagine her intuition as Santa Claus. She found him to be a comforting character that she could turn to easily in times when she needed some sage advice to consider along with her logic, advice from friends, and the results of her research on the topic. She had fun with this when she was shopping for a new dining table and, after priming her intuition, asked Santa Claus what he would pick.

Get Out of Your Head and Into Your Body

James is a former performing artist and loves to be playful. For his priming exercises, we usually pick something silly and have fun with it. In one of our sessions, he wanted to ask his intuition a loaded question about his relationship with his girlfriend, which he was very stressed about. I could sense that he was nervous about the answer he might get.

I had James stand up and walk around as if the floor was covered in sand. He placed all his attention on his feet. After a few minutes, we changed it to the floor being covered with something sticky. We went through a few other imaginary surface coverings, including cake frosting. Pretty soon, he was laughing and having a great time. When I sensed that he was relaxed enough, and his conscious mind wasn't mulling over the relationship question, I had James stop and do his intuition gesture, ask his question, and capture the first answer he got in response. I told him to ask his intuition for clarification with a follow-up question, if needed. The answer he received was that he was standing in the way of this relationship getting deeper because of his own fears. We talked about how he could put this together with what his logic was saying and ponder these inputs carefully to decide on his next steps.

Some of my students come in pairs or trios. One mother-daughter duo got a kick out of a priming exercise that involved mud. I asked them what they loved to play with, and this was their answer. I had them close their eyes and imagine playing with mud, making pots or shapes and even painting their arms and faces with it. This was a great way for them to get out of their heads. When they seemed to be relaxed with all the fun and play they were experiencing, I had them ask their questions, which they'd prepared ahead of time. Both of them got useful insights—the mother about her future career plans and the daughter about her science project. This is a great reminder that you're never too young or too old to access your intuition—and to have fun doing it.

Check Your Intuition Inbox

If you work well with an organized schedule and learn and perform better when you plan, create a special slot on your calendar every day for intuition time. Try to pick a time when you can be in a relatively quiet space for five to ten minutes. Every day when your daily intuition time comes, sit or lie down comfortably, take a few deep breaths, do a quick priming exercise, and ask your intuition if it has any messages for you that day.

You can think of this as checking your voicemail, email, or text messages. You make time to check those multiple times a day, so just five minutes for checking in with your intuition should be doable, especially if you prioritize it in your calendar. Record the messages you get in your journal to be able to refer back or meditate on them later.

In his book *Tiny Habits*, Stanford University's Behavior Design Lab founder and director Brian J. Fogg explains how one of the best ways to build a new habit is to anchor it atop another habit that you already have. If you are someone who doesn't tend to set or follow schedules, you can tie your intuition check-in time to another daily habit of yours, such as brushing your teeth. You can sit or lie down for a few minutes each morning or evening after you brush your teeth. If you have fifteen minutes, you can do the sacred space meditation to check in with your intuition. If you don't have much time, you can brush your teeth mindfully by bringing all your attention to the sensations of the toothbrush touching your gums, or the taste of the toothpaste. As your conscious thoughts calm down, you can check in with your intuition and ask if it has any advice for you for the day ahead.

Maybe you can tie a quick intuition check-in to the habit of checking your emails or text messages at specific times of the day. Ask your intuition if it has any messages for you yet. You can even imagine a screen similar to the one on your phone or laptop where the messages appear.

Some of my clients and students like to check their intuition inbox in the evening before they go to sleep. They keep their intuition journal on their nightstand in case they have intuitive moments from the day that they'd like to record. This practice makes them review the day through their inner wisdom, which can help increase self-awareness, compassion, and gratitude. What a great way to say good night.

Bedtime Receptivity

Keep your intuition journal by your bedside—you can also use your phone's notes app. Before you go to bed, write down a question that you would like your intuition's input on. Set it aside on your nightstand or any other place that would be within reach when you wake up. As soon as you wake up, open it and look at your question; pay attention and capture the first thought, feeling, or sensation you have. (You can also combine this exercise with checking your intuition inbox at the end of the day.)

Since sleep will prime you nicely (unless you were not feeling well and had a disturbed slumber), your intuition will be ready when you are waking up. This also works during the minutes before sleep, when you're in that half-awake state. If you have a voice recorder or your phone next to you, it would be easy to capture your intuitive messages without having to fully wake up.

For people who say they're likely to forget about the question in the morning, I suggest writing it on a piece of paper, crumpling it up, and putting it on the floor right where their feet will go in the morning when they get up, as a reminder.

My student Joanna loves to do this, especially on weekends, when she asks her intuition fun questions, such as: "Where should I hike tomorrow?" or "Which friend should I contact for an impromptu catch-up?" She says that she gets great ideas about relaxing ways to spend her weekends when she checks in with her intuition.

Doodle to Prime

Pam had spent years caring for her mom, and after her passing a few months ago, Pam felt a profound void—not just emotionally, but physically too. With so much extra time and energy on her hands, she wasn't sure where to focus it.

As we were wrapping up our session, she asked me what she could do to fill that space. I suggested she write down her question and doodle around it, letting her thoughts wander freely. This playful exercise helped Pam prime her intuition, guiding her on how to honor her mom's memory while also allowing herself to grieve. As she doodled little flowers, she remembered how much her mom loved them. Inspired, she decided to volunteer at a nearby public garden, helping care for the flowers there.

You can try this technique for yourself the next time you have a question for your intuition. Write your question down and add some fun doodles around it, maybe using colored pencils. You can even make the question mark huge and fill it in, just like a coloring book. Let your thoughts drift as you get lost in the colors and shapes. When you feel calm and your mind is quieter, look at your question and see what insights come through. As always, thank your intuition for the guidance and double-check it with your logical mind before acting on it.

For another playful twist, try drawing or painting a picture to prime your intuition. Don't worry about making it perfect—just let it flow. You could draw a simple house, a tree, mountains, or the sun in the sky. Close your eyes and imagine stepping into the scene you've created. Bring all your senses into it—feel the textures, smell the air, hear the sounds, and notice the colors and shapes around you. Once you feel fully immersed, drop your question into the scene and see what unfolds. Maybe a dog delivers you a message in a bottle, or you find an envelope with the answer inside, or you just know the answer without knowing how.

My student Mehmet tried this by drawing a mountain cabin; then, he imagined visiting it with his teenage son. When he felt completely present in the scene, he asked his intuition how he could be a better father. The answer came through clearly: allow his son to be himself more. Mehmet realized that he and his son were more alike than he had thought, both valuing authenticity and freedom.

Key Takeaways

- Tapping into your intuition on demand takes practice, but there are plenty of fun and easy priming exercises that can help you to do so—and you can also make up your own.
- Often, it is easier to quiet your mind when you are or can imagine yourself in a safe, sacred space.
- Activating a flow state, which helps you lose track of time in a pleasurable way, is a wonderful method of accessing your inner wisdom.
- Getting your intuitive juices flowing by taking a walk is another great way to tune in to what your intuition has to communicate to you.
- Your intuition can also be thought of as your inner light, and visualizations and meditations that help you access this comforting, peaceful, healing light can sensitize you to messages from your intuition.
- The soothing and restorative qualities of water can help provide the kind of clearing energy that's ideal for priming.
- Literally emptying out your thoughts and mental habits through your breath and intention can make you more receptive to your inner guidance.

- As many traditions the world over can attest to, paying attention to the flow of your breath is a wonderful way to calm your mind and emotions, and to attune to your intuition.

- Sometimes, it can be easier to imagine that your intuition has its own persona, like a wise individual, that you are capable of dialoguing with to receive answers to questions you might have.

- Using fun, playful exercises to get out of your conscious thinking and into your body is a great way of relaxing and calming yourself, and thus, of accessing your inner wisdom.

- Just as you might check emails and text messages multiple times a day, make a habit of checking your intuition "inbox," even if it's only for five minutes a day. You can make this process even simpler (and easier to remember and prioritize) if you anchor it to another daily habit, such as brushing your teeth.

- Practice accessing your intuition at bedtime by journaling about your intuitive insights throughout the day and also dropping a question into your journal or a piece of paper that you can then "answer" with the first thought, knowing, or sensation you receive in the morning as you wake up.

- Doodling is another great way to prime your intuition because it allows your mind to relax and wander freely. By letting your hand move without rigid expectations, you create a playful space where intuitive thoughts can surface with greater ease.

Reflections

- Which of the priming practices in this chapter did you feel the strongest connection to? What made them stand out? How can you begin incorporating these into your life on a regular basis?

- Were there certain activities you don't feel as comfortable practicing? Why might that be? (Knowing the reason can give you insight into methods of accessing your intuition that work for you; for example, I have students who prefer the meditation exercises to the ones that are more connected to daily activities.)

- Did the chapter give you any ideas about priming exercises of your own (perhaps related to activities you already do or activities you'd like to try)?

- In many ways, priming for intuition works best when we are engaged with activities and practices that we enjoy and that put us in a relaxed, open, and quietly curious state. Brainstorm a list of activities and practices that fit this criterion and think of ways you can use them to prime for intuition.

CHAPTER 5

Diving Past Linear Logic—How Your Inner Wisdom Speaks in Metaphors and Symbols

Lots of students come to me with questions regarding the significance of some of the messages they receive from their priming and tuning-in attempts. Sometimes, they won't get a clear response, but something that tugs at the corners of their emotions and memories, often in the form of a symbol: a butterfly, a beautiful object, the strains of a song that used to have great meaning for them. When they ask me what such information is conveying to them, I always respond, "What does it mean to you?" and encourage them to ask this question to their intuition.

When we are dealing with subtler forms of information, it's a good idea to receive them without getting overly analytical, logical, or linear. Often, symbolic information in the form of sound, imagery, or any other sensory impressions has many different associations that might make the idea of a single interpretation less relevant. In addition, working with our intuition is not about finding a final answer. Every message we receive, symbolic or otherwise, leads to another message. It's like a breadcrumb along the path of our life journey.

Throughout this chapter, I also emphasize how important it is to attune ourselves to the language of symbols when it comes to working with our intuition. Our nonconscious processing mind, which is where our intuition lives, doesn't use a specific language. It also shows up in different ways for different people. Accessing vast amounts of information stored in our subconscious or unconscious, the insight, idea, or answer that pops up can sometimes be summarized in the best possible way as a symbol or a metaphor.

For example, when tuning in to a new potential destination for a trip you'd like to take, you may get a giant X, which might be telling you not to go there, or the image of a hedgehog, which could be related to a prickly situation or a sign of interesting things you might see there. The interpretation of a symbol or metaphor you receive can often come about when you check back in with your intuition, especially if you're not certain. You can pick the first explanation that comes to you and simply ask your intuition if your interpretation is correct or not.

Overall, metaphors and symbols are great gateways to intuition. They can help us move from conscious analytical thinking to the nonconscious process of intuition. At the same time, we also prime ourselves by slowing down our conscious thoughts, which tend to be ruminations on the usual subjects and suspects we have in mind. Exploring symbols and metaphors can relax us.

Metaphors as Cognitive Tools

In their seminal book *The Metaphors We Live By*, cognitive linguist George Lakoff and his coauthor Mark Johnson explore the importance of metaphors in our lives. They put forth the idea that metaphors are fundamental to how we think, perceive, and act in the world. Their famous conceptual theory suggests that metaphors are part of an extensive unconscious system that structures our thoughts and experiences.

Since intuition involves unconscious processing, it is closely related to how we connect to metaphors, which can act as a bridge to our inner wisdom. This bridge can also help us understand why metaphors are often used in various forms of therapy and coaching. As explained in Jill A. Stoddard and Niloofar Afari's *The Big Book of ACT Metaphors*, they can be used to explore problems, gain insights, and help us see situations from different perspectives, as they not only access the conscious but can also reach the subconscious and unconscious.

Tapping into your intuition for insights into life's challenges can support you in self-coaching, along with using your intellect to figure out what to do and how to be. A simple way of doing this is to gently contemplate what metaphor or symbol best represents the situation. Then, you can connect with that metaphor or symbol with all your senses, imagining how it would look, feel, sound, and smell; its temperature and texture; and so on. If and when you find yourself consciously analyzing the metaphor or symbol, you could pause and go back to working with your senses rather than consciously thinking about what it means or what it's like.

For example, if a tangled ball of yarn shows up in your imagination as a response, you can hold this image in your mind for a while, bringing all your attention to discovering the details. What are the colors and types of yarn that make up the ball? How big or small is it? You can even imagine what this ball smells like, how it feels to the touch, and so on. You can observe with a childlike curiosity, without analyzing or judging. When you feel relaxed and your logical mind is quiet, you can ask your intuition what this ball represents, if it needs to be detangled, and if so, what would help—and any other questions that arise for you.

Serena saw a lock inside her heart during a meditation I was guiding her through. I had her connect with the image by paying attention to the details. We went through what it looked and smelled like, the sounds it would make, its temperature and texture, and so on. It was a thin little lock, easy to break even if it did not open with a key—or maybe the key was lost. When she felt ready, Serena asked the lock what it symbolized. The answer she received was about her feelings of unworthiness. I suggested she ask a follow-up question— the first one that popped into her mind. She inquired as to where she could start to heal; she received insight that she could spend more time with people who appreciated her and less time with those who took her for granted. She was especially grateful and happy about how we deeply connected to the symbolic information rather than simply letting it pass. She was used to meditation journeys that largely ignored such details rather than revisit them.

As I mentioned before, metaphors and symbols can be powerful coaching tools. In addition to working with intuition, I am also a life and executive coach. Metaphors are used in coaching to dig up insights into people's work and life challenges. Coaching is all about asking questions to help the client find areas they may want to consider making changes to improve their lives, relationships, and performance. Sometimes, coaching clients are so wrapped up in their problems and situations that it can be hard for them to see the obstacles they may be able to remove and shifts they can make. Using a metaphor can help them see through all this.

Coaches can offer a metaphor or ask the client to come up with their own. For example, if a client says their work project is daunting, and they don't know where to start, a coach can offer a metaphor that compares this daunting situation to walking in a dark cave. They can also ask the client to feel in to what a more appropriate metaphor might be. Once they have a metaphor, the coach goes through a process of helping the client by asking questions to reveal insights that enable them to move forward. Intuition plays a key role here. The coach supports the client to access their intuition to help them go deeper into the situation so that they can sort through what is possible.

Metaphors are a great way of priming for intuition, as they open up the mind and the heart by creating a healthy mental and emotional distance from the current troubling situation. Even people who are very literal have can find metaphors highly useful. If you ask someone what they're feeling when they're stuck in a situation, they may not be able to articulate it. However, if you offer some metaphors to get them going, such as, "Do you feel stuck like a bird is stuck in a cage?" you can help them get out of their conscious thinking into a deeper place within themselves.

As we deepen into the metaphors, we deepen our priming. Similarities and patterns help our intuition come alive. When you are trying to tune in to someone, you can ask your intuition silly interview questions about them, such as, if they were a fruit, what fruit would they be and why? The key is to do this without thinking about the answer and capturing the first thing that pops up.

Colors as Metaphors

We can use colors to have our intuition speak to us. When you are trying to tune in to someone after priming yourself, try to imagine what color would be around them. This is not about reading their aura, or the energy field around a person. It is a simple technique for using a color as a metaphor, which you can later explore in depth.

Let's say you imagine that a friend has green around them. Tune in to this color further. Is it light or dark green? Is it clear or opaque? Sparkly or textured? Ask your intuition what this color is telling you about this person. Does it reflect their personality or their emotional state? What do the details in the color represent?

You can do this for yourself, as well. When you are having a hard time figuring out how you feel about a situation, prime yourself before asking your intuition what color or colors would be around you now. When you get a color, ask your intuition what it represents and even what the cause might be. We're not talking about color theory or logically analyzing the colors here; it's really more about what that color means to you in that moment. But there may still be nonconscious connections to certain colors and traditions. For example, someone who grew up thinking of red as the color associated with danger might see red when her intuition is warning her about her safety. Another person who grew up learning that red is the color of luck and prosperity could see or feel red around them when their intuition is delivering the message that auspicious things are coming.

What's on the Flip Side?

My coaching client Omar was feeling stuck in his work and life. Any potential step we discussed in any direction seemed impossible to him. I asked him to choose a good metaphor for what was standing in his way. He said it was a mountain. I had him imagine the details of this mountain, such as its size, colors, texture, shapes, angles, and vegetation. This helped to prime him and connected him more deeply with the metaphor.

After we played with bringing some of the details of this mountain to life, I asked, "If this mountain had a word or a few words written on it, what would they be?" He immediately got the word *control*. I told him to imagine that he could magically transport himself to the other side of this mountain and explore. He said that the word *adventure* was written on that side. The colors were brighter, and the air felt fresher.

Omar later told me that the letters of the word *control* were neat and tidy, whereas the word *adventure* had a lot of playfulness in it, with different colors and shapes around the letters, and did not line up perfectly. We ran this through the filter of his logic and talked about how his intuition might be telling him to explore further in the areas where he was maintaining, or attempting to maintain, a tight control.

This exercise is very useful when it comes to exploring possibilities, especially when someone is only seeing what's in front of them or their current situation. Usually, the tendency to only see what's directly present comes from our own self-sabotaging mode. Exploring through metaphors can allow us to find ways around our self-sabotage and the seeming obstacles that arise from it. We can be assured that another way truly is possible.

Of course, whatever is on the flip side will have specific meaning to us. Someone else who initially sees the word *control* might encounter family or connection on the other side, which could signify the importance of being with their loved ones. It's also possible to receive only a sense of what the word on the flip side means when we ask our intuition about it. Staying in the intuition realm helps ensure that we aren't allowing our judgments and preferences to color our interpretation. You can go deeper into the meaning by priming, then asking follow-up questions to your intuition.

Image or Symbol on a Person

If you're having a hard time tapping into your intuition about a person (which we'll discuss in greater depth in chapter 7), you can try to go about it through a metaphor. After priming yourself for intuition, you can imagine that person in front of you: allow a symbol, image, or other metaphor that represents what you are trying to tune in to arise on or around that person, or between you.

Carmina was wondering about her dad's emotions around a family dispute that had been going on for months. Her dad had never been very communicative and closed in even more when there was a conflict. After priming, I had Carmina imagine her dad standing in front of her; then, I asked if she noticed a shape, image, or object around his heart, which is the symbolic center for our emotions (just as the head or forehead tends to be associated with our thoughts and cognition).

Carmina saw a swirling vortex over his chest. I had her pay close attention to this vortex and notice the colors, the movement, and anything around it. Once she was very connected to this image, I had her ask the vortex directly what it meant so her intuition could speak through it. She got that it was about the fear of losing people. When we talked about this later and ran it through the filter of her logic, she confirmed that it made sense, based on her father's tendencies.

When you want to receive intuitive insights about what's going on in someone's heart or mind, or between you and them, you can imagine a symbol, shape, or object over that part of their body or in between you. You can watch it in your mind's eye by bringing all your attention there, letting thoughts go and not analyzing, and just noticing the details. Again, receive all the details before asking your intuition what all of it means. You can capture the first things that come to you and later run them through the filter of your logic.

What Is the Gift?

When you are puzzled about what the lesson is in a situation or a relationship, you can try this exercise, which works under the premise that there is a gift hiding beneath the surface.

After you settle in a comfortable place and relax with deep breathing, imagine that a cloud comes and lifts you up and takes you to a place that represents this situation. Bring all your senses into this scene and make it come alive with visual details, smells, sounds, textures, temperature, and so on.

If this is about a situation, such as a meeting at work, you can imagine going to the meeting room or your own office. If it is about a relationship, you can imagine meeting that person at a café or park. If you are tuning in to a situation such as the work meeting, imagine finding a box waiting for you on the conference table or on your desk at your office. Allow yourself to be playful and creative, and imagine all the details of the box, including how heavy or light it feels when you lift it.

Open the box, which feels very much like a gift, and see what is inside. This may be an object, a word, or even something symbolic, such as a stone. You can pick it up or leave it in there, following your intuition. Tune in to the object, word, or symbol. Observe it; notice how it looks, smells, sounds, and feels to the touch. When you feel connected to it and nicely primed, ask your intuition what it means.

If you are tuning in to a relationship with a person, simply imagine them giving you a box with a gift in it at your meeting place, then go through the same steps to explore and receive its meaning. Note the messages with the intention of remembering them. Then, bring your attention back to your current physical environment, feeling where you are sitting or lying down. Move your arms, legs, fingers, and toes, and slowly flutter open your eyes.

When I guided Adrian through this exercise during a time when he was experiencing friction with his manager, his intuition showed him a certificate inside an envelope on his desk. He immediately recognized this as the certification of the training he had been wanting to sign up for. He had been shying away from doing this, as it meant he'd need to take some time off from work. He didn't even want to risk upsetting his manager by asking. His intuition, however, was encouraging him to explore the possibility. He ran this through his logic and decided to take action. His manager was actually pleased about him taking the initiative, and their work relationship was smoother after he came back from the training.

Symbolic Clichés Work Just as Well

Rick wanted to tap into his intuition about some advice on how to approach his teenage daughter, who was reacting to his recent divorce from her mom. I told him how using symbols and metaphors helped us move from conscious, linear thinking to our inner knowing by seeing the entire picture from many angles. I explained how he could use even symbolic clichés, such as doors, windows, keys, and so on, to observe the behavior of the people in his life. (Again, we'll get into more people-related exercises in chapter 7.)

I asked Rick to pick an imaginary space that would be comfortable for him and his daughter to meet. He said it would be a living room, which for him was a symbolic site of resolution and connection. First, he imagined himself sitting on the sofa. Then, his daughter arrived and picked a place to sit. He observed where and how she sat, as well as what she said out loud and with her body language. Rick saw his daughter choosing a separate chair and facing him sideways. Her body language revealed love for her dad, but also hesitation and confusion around what to do with some of her frustration related to her parents' divorce.

Here is another cliché that can help. If you are about to take on a new challenge, you can imagine it as a door or a gate. Then, observe the details. What is this door or gate made of? Does it look old or new? Is it hard or easy to open? As you receive more and more details and write them in your journal, you can ask your intuition what each of these representations means. For example, perhaps the door creaking loudly and being heavy and hard to open can demonstrate that this endeavor is a difficult one. Run whatever details and messages you receive through the filter of your logic before making any ultimate decisions.

Healing Image Meditation

This is an exercise to practice communicating with your intuition through metaphors in a gentle and fun way. Have a piece of paper or your journal and a pen ready to take notes or to draw on after this guided meditation.

1. Sit or lie down in a comfortable position in a quiet place where you will not be interrupted or disturbed by external stimuli. Please note that if you are interrupted or lose your concentration, you can always go back to following your breath. Then you can restart the meditation or gently bring it to the end if you need to take a break and start later. There is no need to stress about making absolutely sure that you won't be disturbed, but try to create a space that will allow you to fully drop in. Turn the ringer off on your phone and close the door of your room if possible.

2. Start by focusing on your breath as it goes in and out. Imagine white and gold or any other beautiful color of light from a source a few feet above flowing in from the top of your head, going through your whole body, and flowing out from the bottoms of your feet and the tips of your fingers, washing any tension or discomfort away.

3. When you feel ready, ask your intuition for a beautiful healing image. Wait a few moments for the image to appear in your mind's eye. This can be a symbol or a shape that you've never seen before, or it can be an object you are already familiar with.

4. When you receive your image, start to explore it. Turn it around fully so you can observe it at different angles, slowly looking at every detail in your imagination.

5. If it is a two-dimensional image, such as a flat circle in a certain color, turn it to the side a bit and look at the back to see if the back is the same color as the front. Maybe there is a healing message written on the back. Do this playfully, as if you are a child peeling off a sticker. Maybe the circle is covering another beautiful layer that is under the first one. Maybe there is a message there. Look at the layer underneath.

6. Maybe the image you get is a complicated one, such as a three-dimensional object or a vessel. Rotate it to look at it from different angles. Notice if it has any cracks or corners. Maybe the object or the vessel is holding a message for you. Again, explore it the way a child would, with joyful curiosity.

7. Tune in to all your senses while exploring your image. There might be particular sounds or even smells. How does the object feel when you touch it? Is it smooth or rough? Is it warm or cold? Does exploring this object leave an interesting taste in your mouth?

8. How about the rest of your body? Does any part of your body connect with this object more than the other parts? What are the sensations in your body that accompany this exploration?

9. When you feel that you have explored this healing image fully, ask the image what healing message it is bringing you. Maybe silence is the message. Whether you receive your healing message now or you received it earlier in the meditation, ask your healing image if it has any other messages to give you before saying goodbye.

10. Pay full attention to notice the message, which may come in many forms. Perhaps a part of the image or object opens up and unfolds to reveal the message, or you hear it, or you receive it symbolically.

11. Whether your message is explicit, symbolic, or silent, receive it and thank your beautiful healing image for appearing and bringing you this message. Put your hand on your heart and say an affirmation that feels right to you, such as, "I thank the universe for this healing experience."

12. Now, bring your attention back to your breath going in and out. Follow your breath for a few cycles.

13. Next, bring your attention to the rest of your body.

Feel where you are sitting or lying down. Start moving your arms and legs gently.

14. When you feel ready, slowly flutter your eyes open and look around. You can gently stretch your arms and legs to feel your body even more distinctly.

15. Record the messages that you received and any other notes about your healing image and symbols in your intuition journal. You can look at your notes any time and ponder these messages. It is best to capture them shortly after this meditation, since our memory can be fleeting.

When I did this meditation with Shannon, she saw a spaceship as her healing image. We had her tune in to what in her life this might be symbolizing. Her intuition was that it represented strangers and unknown things, which typically made her very cautious. The message she received was that she could actually explore more new things and have fun while still being careful.

Secret Library Meditation

You can use this meditation to find the reason something is the way it is or any other question you have for your intuition. You can do this anytime to gain insight into the reasons for events or situations in your life. This is not coming from the assumption that every bad thing happens for a good reason. First of all, you can do this meditation to look into the reasons for the good things in your life, as well as the more challenging things. Going into why you have some good things in your life can serve to inspire and motivate you.

This work can also show you how to create or invite more good things into your life. If you would like to gain insight regarding how you can turn a difficult event or situation in your life into something better that serves a higher purpose, you can also use this meditation.

1. Settle in a comfortable, quiet place. Take a few deep breaths and bring your attention to the air around you. Let that air be filled with light; a ball of that light lifts you up and gently floats you away in time and space.

2. Imagine landing softly in a beautiful place in nature. Let the magic ball of light open up as you step out onto the ground.

3. Feel the ground beneath your feet. Start noticing the details of the scenery around you. Maybe there are many trees, maybe just a few. Perhaps there are clouds in the sky and children playing in the distance.

4. Find a path that feels inviting and let it lead you to a beautiful building. Imagine the details of this building. Is it old or new? Angular or rounded? Brick or wood or cement? What are the colors and textures?

5. As you walk toward it, let more details come into focus as the building takes shape before you. The building has a big door at the front where the path ends. See every detail of this building as you come closer.

6. You notice a placard over the door that says Your Library. As you approach the door, take a confident step over the threshold as you know you created this

building and there can only be good things inside for you. Feel your curiosity about the wealth of information and insights you will find in this beautiful library.

7. Now you are inside the library. It is filled with light and shelves and shelves of beautifully bound books. There are big desks with comfortable chairs around them to sit and read.

8. As you find yourself in this amazing library, you remember a question you've been holding for some time around why a particular event or situation exists in your life. As you think of this question, just like the lights in a movie theater guide you where to walk, a path lights up toward a specific point on one of the big shelves. You walk toward this shelf, where a small spotlight points to a specific book.

9. You take a deep breath as you affirm that you are ready to know the reasons for the event or situation in your life, and that this library only contains helpful information to guide you toward positive insights.

10. Pick up the book from the shelf and look at it. Feel the hard cover and see the colors. You can even smell that familiar scent that all your favorite books have.

11. Take the book with you and walk to one of the desks. You sit down on one of the comfortable chairs. Then, you open the book and confidently pick a page and paragraph, allowing yourself to be guided to the information that you need.

12. Right there in front of you are the words and pictures to explain to you an important insight about the question you've been holding in your mind. As you

look at the words and the images, which may include pictures or beautiful ornamental design around the letters, you start to see the letters coming together to form an insightful message for you and answering your question about the reasons for the specific event or situation in your life.

13. You look at this message and run your fingers over it. You sit on that chair with this beautiful book open in front of you for a few moments to let your mind, body, and spirit fully absorb this insight. Notice how you feel, receiving this wisdom.

14. When you feel ready, slowly stand up and return the book to its place on the shelf. As you slide the book back in place, you thank it and this library for providing you with a clear answer.

15. Look around one more time and say goodbye to this library, knowing you can come back here anytime you want to get an answer to a question about yourself, your relationships, your work, or your life—or any other questions you might have.

16. Slowly walk back outside through the door you entered. As you stand on the path that led to the library, you are enveloped in a refreshing breeze that brings a swirl of light. This light surrounds you and forms a beautiful ball that lifts you up, so you are floating in time and space.

17. Now, the ball of light gently brings you back to your current physical environment. Feel where you are sitting or lying down. Gently move your hands and feet, your shoulders, and your arms and legs.

18. When you feel ready, gently flutter open your eyes. Look around and reorient yourself to where you are.

19. Take out your intuition journal and write down the message that you received in the library. You can also write down your impressions and emotions, and any other insights that follow.

Key Takeaways

- Often, symbolic information in the form of sound, imagery, or other sensory impressions has a lot of different associations that can expand our interpretations of whatever we're consulting our intuition about. In addition, intuition can often speak to us in the language of symbols and metaphors.

- As many researchers have concluded, metaphors are fundamental to how we think, perceive, and act in the world. They're part of a fundamental unconscious system that structures our experience of ourselves and others, as well as the meaning we give to the events and situations in our lives.

- Colors have symbolic meanings that can offer us a pretty immediate sense of what our intuition is trying to communicate, based on how the color makes us feel and what we might naturally associate with it.

- When we feel stuck, or when we can only see what's right in front of us, imagining what's on the flip side of the situation can help us envision more possibilities and experience a greater sense of agency.

- Symbols, images, and metaphors can offer us a great

deal of insight about our relationships with the people in our lives, especially if we are unable to communicate in more direct ways.

- Situations and relationships that puzzle us can be seen as metaphorical gifts in the form of boxes or envelopes with specific symbolic messages inside them.

- Our symbols and metaphors don't have to be complicated. Clichés work just as well as more complex and involved symbols and metaphors—and we can use them to great effect in our intuitive exercises.

- If you are in doubt about something in your life or you simply seek an uplifting message, you can always ask your intuition for a healing image and use the meditation in this chapter to do so.

- If you want to better understand the how or why of a situation in your life or in the world, imagine a beautiful library. In this library, a passage in a specific book is there to shed light on your situation. This can be a very powerful and intuitively stimulating meditation.

Reflections

- What is your relationship to symbols and metaphors? Do they help invoke your intuitive faculties? Or do you have difficulty with material that isn't literal?

- If you have difficulty interpreting symbols, try using your intuition to ask additional questions that garner insight, rather than forcing a specific interpretation onto the symbols and metaphors that arise. When you ask your intuition for more insight, what happens?

- What symbols and metaphors have special meaning to you? Can you use the exercises in this chapter to braid them into your intuitive practice?
- Which of the exercises in this chapter piqued your interest? What made them appealing?

CHAPTER 6

Through New Eyes—Discovering Intuition in Everyday Objects

Everyday objects can work just like symbols and metaphors and become gateways to intuition. We can use them to help prime ourselves for intuition by bringing all our attention to exploring them one sense at a time. We can pick objects that are associated with the person or situation we would like to tune in to, then let our intuition speak through them to pick up insights about this person or situation. We can also interact with objects to gain a sense of connection to the past or to people who are no longer around. This is not for the purpose of mediumship, but for distilling powerful lessons or advice from our own intuition. Finally, we can connect with an object that gives us messages about life and our surroundings that we might not have expected.

A simple way to work with objects is to look for them around the room or the outdoor space you are in. Take deep breaths and allow your gaze to scan the environment casually, letting thoughts and judgments go and just observing. When you see something that draws your attention more than anything else, start looking at it as if you are seeing it for the first time. If it's an object you can hold, bring your attention to the sensation of touch and explore it with your hands and fingers, with childlike curiosity. Next, you can go into the sense of smell, followed by exploring if it makes any sound when you move it or tap on it. This helps you connect with the object while also priming yourself. After this exploration, you can hold the object near your heart or gut, depending on where you feel your intuition more. Next, close your eyes and ask the object what it would like to say to you. Try to capture the first thing that pops up in your mind and make a note of it. If it is a symbolic response, such as a shape or an image, you can go deeper into that with your intuition and ask what it means.

When we tried this with Carla, her attention was drawn to a plant. After exploring it with all her senses, I asked her what this plant would tell her if it could talk. She said it would have reminded her of her strength and told her to keep her head up as she rebuilt her life. She had just lost her job and appreciated these words of encouragement from her own intuition. She had taken good care of that plant, but it had almost wilted away to make a comeback later. The combination of her history with the plant and her subconsciously knowing that she was strong and would take care of herself came together in this beautiful message.

Another student, Tanya, had her attention drawn to a window with closed curtains during this exercise. She looked at the window, observed it casually, and let conscious thoughts and judgments go. When I asked her what the message of this window was, she said it was about noticing the beauty behind something instead of only seeing what is on the surface. I asked her to check in with her intuition regarding how this related to something in her current life. She said it was about her son. Her intuition was telling her to let go of expectations and judgments about his life and notice the beauty behind the surface.

Just remember, similar to the metaphors we explored in the last chapter, an object works as a conduit that helps us connect to our subconscious or unconscious—to what we already know deep down but what has not yet surfaced. We can work with an object to connect with our intuition, search for answers, and help those answers percolate up to our awareness.

Talking to Everything

I was born a talker. I started to speak very early in life, and I have been talking to everything ever since. What I mean by "talking" here is actually communication that includes quiet chats with myself and my intuition. As a toddler, I used to talk to my food, asking each vegetable on my plate for permission to eat it. I talked to my chair after sitting on it for too long or dropping myself down onto it too hard. I asked if it was tired and apologized for not being more thoughtful.

As I grew up, this chatter became quieter. It still continued, but it became more of an internal dialogue. In my twenties, I remember having fun with this tendency while out shopping. You know that feeling when you're in a store and you find one thing you love. You pick it up, hold it, and consider putting it in your cart. Then, something stops you. In my case, I'd end up having an internal dialogue with whatever the object was: "I am very affected by you. I think I love you, but I'm just not sure if it's the right time to take our relationship to the next level. If you come home with me now, I'm afraid of our love not holding up later. Then you may think I didn't respect you, it was all a waste, and you could have been put to better use with someone else."

I always believed that everything had a character, in the sense that I recognized the creative force of the universe that ran through all objects, animate or inanimate. Every object was an amazing collection of creative energy bundled together in some fascinating form or another. The chair had pieces of wood from the trunk or branches of a tree. It had upholstery that was woven from various sources, such as cotton that grew in the fields or polyester that came from petroleum. People worked on each of these materials to put them in new forms and shapes, and to give them new properties. As they created each piece in their own way, their essence intertwined with the essence of each material, formed a new amalgamation, and gave the object a character.

Some people can easily feel this when they look at or hold a work of art. I believe it is true for every object that can be traced back to living materials, which covers pretty much everything around us.

Talking to everything does not mean sitting and having a conversation with the chair and the coffee table, although that might be fun if you happen to be really bored. Talking to everything means paying due respect to all objects, since considerable energy went into their formation. It means loving even the stone that bothers you when it's stuck in your shoe and removing it with respect and at least a bit of awe about its creation. It means pulling or shaking it out, saying quietly to yourself, "What are you doing in there, you silly little thing? Here—you're free now," instead of getting frustrated and throwing it out with anger.

When I gave Hilda the exercise of talking to everything, she first thought I was joking. Then she approached it with an open mind and came back to the next lesson smiling widely, saying that she felt love for even the most random objects, such as her toothbrush, after trying this.

This exercise is all about coming from the heart in every action and interlacing everything we do with love. I truly believe that our purpose in life is to love and be loved, to spread compassion wherever we go and in whatever we do. We are such amazing forms of creation, and so is everything else in the universe. When we live our life from the heart, with compassion for ourselves and those around us, then we truly feel fulfilled and at peace. Research from the HeartMath Institute reveals how syncing your heart and mind unlocks powerful intuition. Their research shows the heart isn't just a pump—it's a super-sensor, picking up on events and sending precognitive signals to your brain before you're even aware of them. As discussed in chapter 2, connecting with compassion opens us up our intuition, and vice versa.

In general, anything you do to increase the vibration of love and compassion increases your ability to stay connected with the universe and everything in it. Love and compassion are what you feel when you connect with the universe. When you are in love with life and all of creation, you are more open to receiving and recognizing intuitive messages. This is true for communication between people as well. When we come from the heart in our words and actions, we're more connected to the people we share our lives with and those with whom we happen to cross paths.

Surprise Objects

Some of my students and clients come in pairs, such as siblings, couples, or friends. This is a particular exercise that works well for two people. To prepare for this exercise, I ask each person to grab an opaque bag or a box, then go for a short treasure hunt during which they choose three objects for their exercise partner that they can fit into this container. When they come back and sit down, I ask them to set aside the bag or box somewhere they can reach easily; then, I ask them to close their eyes and start breathing deeply, noticing all the sensations associated with their breath.

When I can see and feel that they are relaxed, I ask them to take turns pulling out one of the objects and handing it to their exercise partner, or dropping it into their lap. Then, I tell each person to hold and feel the object that was just given to them. This is done by feeling the surface and nooks and crannies of the object with their hands, and paying full attention to every detail while still keeping their eyes closed.

After a few moments of this exploration, I ask them to put the object near their ears and move or rotate it between their fingers or palms, then shake and tap on it to check if the object makes any sound. Then, I tell them to bring the object near their nose, smell it, and focus only on that sensation. The next step is to bring the object close to their mouth and imagine how it would taste—without actually biting into it, of course. Next, they open their eyes and look at every detail of this object with their full attention, letting judgments go and seeing the object through the eyes of a curious little kid. Then, I ask them to close their eyes again and hold the object over their heart or abdomen and just feel it; from here, they ask the object a question, like, "Is there anything you would like to tell me?" and capture the response. Once this feels complete, they hand each other the next object and repeat the same process until they have gone through all three objects.

Finally, they conclude by grounding themselves by feeling where they are sitting and gently fluttering open their eyes to complete the exercise. After my students open their eyes, I ask them if there were surprises, and whether the meaning of any of the objects changed for them with this exercise. Some of them report having long, soul-searching conversations with the objects.

Then, I ask my students why they think we did this exercise, and how they felt about it. Most of them immediately recognize that this exercise is for priming and accessing their intuition while awakening all their senses as much as possible. It's also an exercise in being mindful and experiencing even simple little things fully. My students also report looking at and treating objects around them differently after this exercise. They seem to have more respect for all the effort, resources, energy, and care that go into creating these objects.

This exercise can even enable nonverbal communication between the exercise partners. I had a pair of students, a brother and sister. He was the younger mischievous one, while she was more serious and taught her brother something at every opportunity. When she connected with the music box he had picked for her as one of her objects, she got the message that she needed to have more fun with her little brother. One of the ways the two siblings enjoyed spending time together was playing their favorite songs on their musical instruments. The box was a reminder of her love for music, as well as the fact that her brother missed these joyful connections. It was an invitation to bring music and joy back into their relationship.

You can try this exercise on your own as well, perhaps with just one object instead of three. Insights are likely to enter your awareness, even without the surprise factor of doing this with a partner.

Meaningful Objects

This is a slightly varied version of the surprise objects exercise that you can do on your own. First prime briefly by breathing deeply with your full attention on your breath, then, following your intuition, find an object to use in this exercise. After you connect with the object through all your senses and priming more deeply by doing so, you can ask the object what it wants to say to you and what made it come forward when you were searching for it.

When Sushir tried this exercise, his intuition guided him to pick his phone charger. After connecting with this little device he used every day but didn't even pay any specific attention to, he received the message that he needed to reach out and see his parents in person soon, instead of relying on video calls to keep in touch with them.

You can also consciously pick an object that is related to an area of your life in which you want guidance from your intuition. You can sit with eyes closed and explore the object with all your senses, one sense at a time, then ask the object what it would like to say to you. Some people gain deep insights from this exercise, as it's a great way to prime and also connect with the essence of the objects.

Carol picked a pair of ceramic baby booties that were given to her by her mom. She was pregnant and wanted to tap into her intuition about how to prepare herself for motherhood. As she held the cute little booties over her heart and asked for advice, her intuition told her to keep researching and reading books about parenting, but also to remember that she would still need to learn by doing when the time came.

Oracle Cards, Inspiring Books, and Rituals

We can use oracle cards or books with healing or inspiring messages to aid our intuition. Sometimes, the messages from our intuition linger at the precipice between our awareness and subconscious or unconscious, waiting to be pulled out with the right prompt. Therefore, card or book readings are best suited to finding inspiration rather than asking yes or no questions.

Oracle cards are especially great for bringing in creativity. Unlike tarot cards, which follow a specific structure, oracle cards are more freeform, with decks varying widely in their themes and interpretations. The playfulness of using the cards and your affinity toward the art and the general theme of the deck are what draw you in, quiet down your conscious thoughts, and relax you. You're letting go and letting the cards take charge. Remember though, that the magic is not in the cards. Exactly which cards you pick doesn't really matter so much. Your own intuition uses the cards as a conduit; the cards become a window through which your intuition can shine its light and illuminate something that inspires you or reminds you of what you already knew deep down.

I like oracle card decks that have positive and healing messages, since I always set the intention of receiving inspiring and constructive messages from my intuition. I have a few different decks of oracle cards and use my intuition to choose the deck that I wish to work with at the moment. I do a quick initial priming, such as deep breathing with my hand over my chest, feeling my breath move in and out gently as I inhale and exhale; after this, I choose the deck that I feel drawn to right away.

Rituals that you can create as you practice tapping into your intuition can later help you prime yourself easily, just as you did when using your intuition gesture. For example, if you pick a favorite quiet corner in your home to try the exercises in this book, after some practice, you can prime yourself by imagining settling into that corner even when you are away from home.

I created a short ritual to help me connect with the cards, which also serves the purpose of priming myself easily. Rituals with beautiful, positive, inspiring components are great ways to prime yourself for intuition. You can create your own ritual or use the following one to guide you.

I fan the deck out and touch each card, bringing all my attention to that tactile sensation and letting thoughts and judgments go. I look at the fanned-out deck with my full attention, taking time to observe the colors and shapes. I place the fanned-out deck over my heart, which is the part of my body I connect most with my intuition; this also brings in my intuition gesture, which is placing a hand over my heart. I set the intention for the card reading in my mind or by saying it out loud. For example, I might say something like, "These cards are bringing me healing, positive messages."

Then, I pull one to three cards and place them face down on a table. Sometimes, I feel called to draw more cards. I turn the first card around and keep my hand on it, with my full attention on that sensation of touch. I observe all the visual details of the art on the card without thinking or judging. I casually scan the words written on it. At this point, I can either pick up the card and put it over my heart or keep my hand on the card and close my eyes, asking what it would like to say to me. I pay full attention to whatever my intuition brings forward as a response. I thank my intuition and the card for this message and move on to the next card, following the same process.

At the end, I check in with my intuition to see if I need to pull any more cards for any follow-up questions I may have related to these messages; then, I go through the same process with those cards. After receiving the individual messages from the cards, I put them back on the table close to each other and place my hands on them to touch all the cards, with my eyes closed. Alternatively, I might hold the cards in my hands and fan them out; then, I bring them over my heart and ask what their collective message is for me.

You can do the same thing with books (again, I prefer positive ones with uplifting, life-affirming messages). To prime yourself, you can first connect with the book by touching its cover and flipping through its pages, with all your attention on observing the sensory details. You can even try bringing the book close to your nose and smelling it, or tapping on it to see if it makes any sounds as you bring it close to your ears. Have fun and use all your senses. These steps are meant to prime your intuition even further and make you feel a personal connection with the book. Then, without looking, flip to a random page—or scan the book and stop at a page that intuitively draws your attention. Pick a paragraph or a sentence, following your intuition. You can take a few deep breaths and read this paragraph or sentence quietly or out loud. If possible, close your eyes and sit with these words, twirling them around in your consciousness for a few moments without analyzing them. If the message in these words is not clear to you, ask your intuition what it means and try to capture the first thing that comes up in response. As always, run this message through the filter of your conscious reasoning before taking any action or making any decision.

When I guided Jake through the oracle-card exercise, he pulled a card that included the words *spark* and *hustle*. The art on the card was painted in yellow and gold. Jake had a difficult health problem that he was dealing with. When he connected to this card deeply by putting his hand on it, observing the visual details, and placing the card over his gut (which he felt was the site of his intuition), he received the message to bring more sparks of excitement into his life so that every day felt less like a hustle. Before selecting a new card, he asked how he could create more excitement. The words *remember who you are*, and the beautiful images on this new card, stimulated Jake's intuition. He remembered that he used to love to sculpt but hadn't done so in a long time. He was inspired to get back to sculpting or some other art form, such as ceramics, that involved a lot of tactile sensation.

Thrift-Store Treasure Hunt

Another playful way of tapping into your intuition through objects is to imagine that you are on a treasure hunt at a thrift store—a place that generally tends to have a plethora of interesting objects to catch your fancy.

After settling into a comfortable place and taking a few deep breaths, close your eyes and let your imagination gently take you to a thrift store or an antique store. Connect with all your senses to bring the scene more and more alive in your mind. Walk around the store and feel your feet touching the floor. Touch surfaces and feel textures and temperatures. Imagine and observe all the visual details, including colors, light, shadows, shapes, angles, lines, and curves. Bring in your sense of smell and imagine what this store or parts of it would smell like. Find objects that can make sounds if you tap on them or move them. Stroll around casually and let your intuition guide you toward a specific object in the scene. Pick it up if you can hold it or come close to it to touch it.

When you feel that you have explored it enough and connected to it deeply, bring it over your heart or gut area, or close your eyes and keep your hands on it. Then ask what it would like to say to you so that your intuition can speak through it. Thank the object and your intuition for this message and gently bring yourself back to your current physical environment. Feel where you're sitting or lying down, move and stretch, and slowly open your eyes.

Jasmine loves thrift shops and was very excited to try this exercise. In the shop she created in her imagination, she found a little wooden sailboat. As she connected with it through her senses in this imaginary scene, she could even feel the delicate strings around the sail and smell the wood it was made of. When she asked what message this sailboat had for her, she got, "Go outdoors and feel the wind in your face." She had been working long hours and had not gone on her beloved beach walks in months. Her intuition was reminding her of the healing effect these walks had on her; it was encouraging her to make time for them once more.

Objects with History

An interesting way of connecting with the wisdom of your ancestors, or even respected figures from history, is to pick an object that you associate with a particular person whose message you'd like to connect with. The idea is that you are using the object and your knowledge of that person's essence to deepen your connection to your own inner wisdom. Once again, this is not an activity that is centered around mediumship, where you are channeling messages from others. It's about recognizing that the things and people we are inspired by can be powerful focal points for accessing those qualities within ourselves.

Many people feel disconnected from their ancestry, or from a sense of connection to the people who came before them. But it's possible to access the wisdom you already have, which is part of the lived experiences of your grandparents, elders, historical heroes, and other people to whom you feel an affinity. We are all connected, and this activity helps us feel that connection tangibly.

Some of my clients do this exercise to connect to the

wisdom of their late parents or grandparents. They hold an object, such as a ring left to them by this ancestor, connect with it through all their senses, and ask for advice. Then, they wait for the message to arrive, in whatever form it chooses to take.

One of my clients, a high school teacher, loves to do this with the picture of the founder of his country; he does so whenever his work feels especially challenging. He uses the picture in his classroom to prime himself. He closely looks at the details of his hero's face and of the scene around him. Once he starts to feel peaceful and his conscious thoughts become quiet, he asks this visionary leader for his advice on the situation. He is always inspired and energized by what his intuition brings forward in response.

Key Takeaways

- Everyday objects can act as intuitive gateways, inviting us to explore them through our senses to prime and connect with our intuition, revealing insights about ourselves, our relationships, and life's deeper messages.
- Communicating with everything around us, from everyday objects to the universe itself, enhances our connection to intuition and to each other.
- You can use objects to engage all your senses, which can help you access intuition, deepen mindfulness, and reveal new insights. This also enhances respect for everyday items and fosters nonverbal connection. You can also have a conversation with an object—much like you'd have with a friend—to surface surprising insights.

- Oracle cards or inspiring books can help bring intuitive messages to the surface, offering guidance and inspiration that may be lingering just below our awareness.
- Another fun way to tap into your intuition through objects is to imagine you're on a treasure hunt in a thrift store—a place often filled with a variety of intriguing items to spark your interest.
- To connect with ancestral wisdom or inspiration from respected historical figures, choose an object associated with them to deepen your connection to inner wisdom, using their essence as a focal point to access those qualities within yourself.

Reflections

- How do you currently relate to the objects around you, and what might shift if you begin to view them as potential gateways to intuitive wisdom?
- Reflecting on a recent symbol or object that caught your attention, what personal meaning or message might it hold for you, and how does it connect to your current life journey?
- When you consider connecting with the essence of an ancestor or admired figure through an object, what qualities or wisdom would you hope to access within yourself?
- How might exploring everyday objects with a sense of curiosity and respect open new pathways to compassion, both for yourself and others?

- If you were to use a tool like oracle cards or a favorite book to inspire intuitive insights, what question or area of life would you like to receive guidance on, and what might your intuition reveal?

CHAPTER 7

Deeper Windows to the Soul—Tuning in to Other People

When you first meet someone, you can pick up many clues about their personality. You can sense how easily you might become friends. Sometimes you feel a warmth toward the person that allows you to sense a shared understanding. Other times you can't wait to get away from someone you've just been introduced to because something about them doesn't feel right to you.

Whether we attribute it to intuition or not, most of us have a gut feeling about the people we encounter on a daily basis, such as something feeling "off" or easily experiencing connection and affinity. Because relationships make the world go 'round, many of my clients and students are especially interested in using their intuition to expand their knowing about specific people in their lives—a new romantic interest, a boss, a colleague, a next-door neighbor, or even a stranger they're curious about getting to know. It's possible to pay attention to our gut feeling and bring it even more deeply into our awareness, so that we can read the people around us for further insight about our connection and our capacity to relate to them.

Just to clarify, we are not talking about mind reading here. First of all, it's impossible to read anyone else's mind with any degree of accuracy—because we usually don't even know what is actually going on in our own heads. Second, intuition about other people is just another way of communicating without language, like when we read nonverbal cues, such as a person's facial expression or their breathing (whether it's shallow or deep, for example).

Verbal communication is great but has its limits and also depends on the person we are interacting with and our connection with them, the mental and emotional state they are in, and so on. A friend may be upset with us about something but not speak about it. Depending on nonverbal cues, we can sense it intuitively and tend to it, repairing the relationship before it's too late. Intuition can give us additional insights, such as feeling a sadness they have, which might be derailing them from their usual behavior. Sometimes people say one thing but mean another, so we can also sense how truthful they're being in addition to consciously noticing this, especially if it's in conflict with other information we have about them. And of course, the information we have can be limited, and we may need to tap into intuition more when we cannot rely on conscious analysis of the data we have "on file."

The exercises in this chapter will help you hone your skill of noticing what's happening beyond the surface so that you can experience more harmonious relationships with the people in your life—or, at the very least, maintain an awareness of what your gut is actually telling you about them.

Nonverbal Cues

Carefully designed research has shown that people are able to decode nonverbal cues to gauge others' emotions, personalities, intentions, attitudes, or skill levels. In 1993, Nalini Ambady and Robert Rosenthal of Harvard University's Department of Psychology ran a study in which students watched a brief video of instructors with whom they'd had no past interaction; the videos were combinations of three ten-second clips taken at various points of a lecture while the instructors were teaching, but they didn't include any sound.

Afterward, students were asked to rate each teacher on their teaching ability. They were also asked to assess each instructor on a variety of characteristics, including whether they were accepting, active, anxious, attentive, competent, confident, dominant, empathic, enthusiastic, honest, likable, optimistic, professional, supportive, and warm. When participants were exposed to shorter silent videos (three clips of two seconds each combined to create a six-second video), their reviews didn't demonstrably change. There was also a high degree of consensus among the participants' ratings. In addition, they were pretty much the same as the ratings by students and a supervisor who'd actually had significant interaction with that teacher, such as taking their class for an entire semester.

The authors of the study concluded that participants knew on an intuitive level whether the teachers they evaluated were adept at what they were doing. Even though the participants may not have been trained in using their intuition, they were primed to pay closer attention than usual, compared to situations when they might have briefly encountered a stranger for a few seconds. As the authors concluded, these findings suggest that "our consensual intuitive judgments" might be accurate—that we seem to communicate (and pick up) a great deal of information about each other nonverbally in a very short time.

When I guided one of my students through an exercise for tuning in to people using photographs rather than videos, she similarly captured several astonishingly accurate insights about those people. When I told her she was spot on, she was very surprised. I asked her how she'd come to these insights, and she said, "I don't know how, but I just knew," a statement people often make when they're talking about their intuition.

In addition to the role of intuition in nonverbal decoding, it also helps with our nonverbal encoding in social or professional situations. Nonverbal encoding is something of a reverse process of decoding. When we need to look confident, we automatically know how to change our body language and our tone of voice. We don't usually do these with a conscious plan, but we intuitively know how a confident person would stand, walk, or sound—and then, we embody some of those attributes. In truth, if we were to consciously plan and assume such roles, unless we were well-trained actors or talented con artists, we'd likely come across as phony. Speaking of actors, many great ones say that even after deliberate planning and preparation for a role, they still rely on their intuition for the right timing and intensity of each gesture and sentence.

Communication with and from the Deeper Self

Many of the exercises in this chapter will help you read another person's energy (essence, character traits, mood, emotions, and so on) for the purpose of improved connection and communication, and give you information that will help you decide how to proceed in the context of your relationship with that person. Sometimes, my clients and students have attempted to read someone else's energy without anything coming through, even after they've done their priming (which should always be done before you attempt any of the exercises to ensure that you are actually connecting with your intuition rather than your conscious thinking—until you can easily distinguish between the two). If this happens to you, just take a few more cycles of deep breaths; if the person you are reading is still in your proximity, glance in their direction quickly, go into your intuition gesture, and drop the question you have about them into the stillness of your mind one more time. Give it a few moments for the answer to come. If you still do not receive anything, it may be the case that this person is not open to nonverbal communication, doesn't like to reveal themselves, and has chosen not to be read. In other words, they may be a closed book with a hard cover and a lock on it. No need to try to pry it open—simply respect their privacy and move on.

Once again, we aren't attempting to read a person's mind or to intrude on their privacy. You don't have to worry about being intrusive, because if someone truly doesn't want to be read, they won't be. Something else to take into account is that when you tune in to someone's energy after priming for intuition, you are communicating at the highest level; that is, your true self is connecting with their true self. If you get hunches, feelings, or intuitive messages about a person's essence, personality, desires, and life experiences, it means that these are being broadcast by that person in the expression on their face; in their eyes; and in the way they sound, stand, walk, and so on.

When I work with students and clients, they are already proverbial open books, because they want to be read. When people come to me for an intuitive consultation for the first time, I tell them that I will most likely reiterate what they already know; at the same time, most people still need to hear it from another person for validation and reassurance. I'm not reading their mind, per se, but I am tuning in to what they are transmitting. When we complete the session and I check if they are satisfied or not, many times they respond, "Yes, I already knew what you said deep down, but I really needed to hear it from you." This helps them increase their self-awareness, taking them deeper into their own inner world.

When I am doing an intuitive consultation for someone, I am actually communicating with that person nonverbally about the things they are aware of on a deeper level that may have been pushed into their subconscious or unconscious. During our session, we do priming exercises together and create a safe place for some of these matters to percolate up to their awareness. When we are both primed, information can flow more easily between us. It's not as easy to read someone who is in an agitated state.

It's important to remember that reading another person isn't a supernatural ability. Human beings are designed to be able to read nonverbal cues. We use this ability in our daily lives without even noticing. Our intuition plays a big role in reading these cues along with our conscious mind. The main difference between how these two styles of assessment operate is whether the conclusions are results of observation followed by judgment and analysis, or impressions that are made immediately without any prior conscious thinking. We are capable of both.

Of course, when our intuition and conscious thinking concur, life is a whole lot simpler. But when they don't, how do we know which one we should trust? We need to be fully aware of our biases and prejudices here so that we can question them. Most of the time, they influence our conscious thinking, especially when it comes to other people, whereas our intuition can paint a different picture—as long as we have learned to catch and interpret it with an open heart and mind.

Relationships can be a source of anxiety for a lot of people, and it's hard to depend on our conscious thinking to tell us accurate stories, especially if we are wired for survival. But tapping into intuition can help us open up to empathy and create space for relationships that aren't so mired in fear and anxiety. When we prime ourselves, as we quiet down the conscious mind, we are also quieting down the survival-based, self-sabotaging tendencies, such as the fear of anyone who is not similar to us. Without the influence of such tendencies, the connection between people can evolve from comparison to the commonalities between us, which creates a greater sense of flow and harmony.

People Practice in Person

The next time you meet someone new, quickly prime yourself and tune in to any impressions or insights you receive about them. You can do an impromptu version of this exercise by trying to read or feel the energies of people you don't know when you're at a public place, such as a restaurant. Don't worry about having to look at people for a long time and making them feel uncomfortable. There is no need to stare. You can just take a quick glance, with the intention of connecting to their energy for the purpose of reading it. You can glance over at them again if necessary as you shift your gaze around. If you have your journal with you, you can take notes or record them on your phone.

You can also do this exercise with people you know, especially as you may not have the opportunity to check your hunches with respect to people you don't know—and this is an exercise that can come in handy for the purpose of shifting from judgment and into a calmer state of mind that allows us to be more open, curious, and receptive toward others. This exercise can help you listen beyond their words and what your conscious mind is capturing. If you ask a friend how they are, and they say "Fine," you can still sense if something is wrong and they are actually not fine, even if this is what they are consciously projecting. We may have less need for this if our experience with that person has been very open and honest, but we can still sense unspoken emotional undertones, which might help us notice things we normally might not. For example, I might say something in a coaching session like, "I am sensing some hesitation here," after a client expresses interest in a new project. They might not have initially felt this way, but often, when they ponder it, they may end up agreeing—and receiving deeper insight into their thoughts and desires.

People Practice with Pictures

You will need a friend or family member to help you with this exercise. Before asking for their help, do some priming so that you are ready to go when they are. Ask your exercise partner to show you a picture of someone whom you have never met and likely never will meet. Look at the picture for a few seconds, letting go of analysis and judgments. Let your partner take the picture away. You can also choose to continue to look at the picture and to keep priming yourself—observing their eyes, face, and other details, as long as you keep conscious analysis and judgment at bay. Capture and share the character traits that come to you about the person in the picture. Blurt it all out and check in with your partner to make sure these were not the results of conscious analysis, judgments, or biases. Have your partner give you feedback on what parts of your observations made sense; refrain from analysis or gossip about the person in the picture. Keep your discussion to what you observed from the picture and what your partner and other people in that person's life can observe easily, since they know them.

After practicing this exercise a few times, try looking only at the eyes of the person in the picture. You can ask your practice partner to zoom in on the picture to show you the eyes only at first. Notice what you get from just the eyes, then move on to looking at the whole face and the whole body. You might be surprised at how much you sense from looking only at the person's eyes. When I tried this with Jason, I told him to blurt out the words that were coming to him. The character traits Jason picked up were: quiet, thoughtful, and curious. All these were accurate. When I showed him the person's whole face, he added: happy, peaceful, and calm. Once again, he was right.

Another student of mine, Robert, was a software-engineering professional who shared from the very beginning that he hoped we wouldn't be meditating or visualizing in our lessons, as he didn't work well with either of those. I told him that we'd focus on priming his intuition with whatever methods worked best for him. In one of our sessions, I gave him the exercise of reading people's character traits from just looking at their photo for a few seconds. He didn't know any of these people, and I didn't give him names or identifying details. In some of the photos, the people were even in costume or removed from the context of their daily lives. Robert became very introspective and began blurting out amazing insights about these people's character traits. He even got very specific, noting their particular sense of humor, their relationships with family, where they were in their careers, and so on. Later, when I asked him if there was any process that had allowed him to receive such accurate insights, he said that he imagined each person in their living room and himself with them; in this scenario, he was telling them a joke and observed the way they reacted, as well as how they interacted with their family and friends. This was surprising, coming from a very analytical person.

Robert's method is a very powerful intuitive technique: simply creating an imaginary scene, putting the person you're reading in it, and observing them. You can even do this with yourself. For example, if you're considering a new job offer, imagine sitting at your desk, being on a Zoom call, or working in a meeting room with the people who interviewed you; tune in to how you feel about this new situation.

Another interesting reaction from Robert, who is also very competitive, was what he said after having gone through many photos. When I was about to show him one last photo, he said he was nervous about this one, given that he had an amazing track record so far and was afraid to ruin it with the final photo. I reminded him that we were not trying to impress anyone—we were just exploring. And if this was a real-life situation, even if he was sure that he was right about a person in terms of that first nonverbal impression, it would be best to run things through his conscious mind or his intellect, as well, to see if they still held—while also giving the other person the benefit of the doubt. This way, he could also try to get to know that person with an open mind.

Nonverbal cues we pick up from others don't always have to be visual; hearing can also play a role. I try the voice-only version of this exercise with some of my students after practicing with pictures a few times. I have them listen to a voicemail from a friend—in Turkish, which these students don't speak. All they have to go by is the tone of the voice they hear. They can still pick up character traits about the person accurately and have an idea about the nature of the message and my connection with that friend.

Tuning in to Someone's Emotional State

In an advanced version of the photo and character-traits exercise, I pull out and focus on images that trigger specific emotions, such as a beautiful countryside that could evoke joy or happiness, and ask my students to tune in to my emotions. I do not share the image with my students and turn my face away if it is an in-person session, or I turn my camera off if it is online, then I speak a few random words unrelated to the image. My students are able to pick up on my emotions when they hear my voice, even if they cannot see my face. I speak with as neutral a tone as possible, yet some of them are able to pick up on subtle emotions.

When I did this exercise with Robert and was looking at the picture of a visual puzzle, he said that he could hear confusion and fascination in my voice but could not explain how or why. This showed him that if he put his full attention and best intentions on the practice, he could replicate it in daily conversations.

This is another useful side effect of getting to know and practicing our intuition. It makes us better listeners. We pay full attention, and as is often said in coaching, we start to listen at level 3. Level 1 listening is when we are actually thinking about what to have for dinner while our friend is telling us about a new project they are excited about. Level 2 is truly listening without thinking about something else. Level 3 is listening to and beyond the words with full attention, also reading nonverbal cues.[4]

---

[4] Many different systems have their own definitions of levels of listening. This one is based on the Co-Active Training Institute's internal, focused, and global levels.

Emotional Memory Exercise for Two People

There is definitely unspoken communication that takes place between two people when they meet, whether they have known each other for a while or not.

This is a fun exercise to see how much we can pick up on someone else's emotional state intuitively and how we are all connected. You can do this exercise with a friend, family member, or practice partner, in person or on a call. To get better results, take time to prime your intuition and calm yourself, emotionally and mentally. Have your partner focus on a memory and imagine reliving it in as much detail as possible. Closing their eyes could help them focus better. The memory doesn't have to be sensational; it can be anything that evokes some emotion in them.

As they are focusing on their chosen memory, set the intention of intuitively tuning in to their emotions. You can look at them or ask them to say a few random words so you can listen to the tone of their voice if you are on a voice-only call. Be alert and catch the first impressions that come to you. Write them down, if you can, or keep them in mind.

Switch your intention and attention to your conscious thinking after doing this and notice what it picks up about your partner's emotional state. Note these thoughts as well. When you feel ready, share what your intuition captured about your partner's emotional state and ask them to give you feedback, and receive it without attachment to being right or wrong. Next, you can discuss what your conscious thinking picked up from them. Observe how your initial intuitive impressions popped up as a knowing or sensation without any preceding conscious thought chain and compare this to your assessments after conscious analysis of your partner's facial expression or tone of voice. How does all of this overlap with your partner's actual emotions?

Pictures Version of the Emotional Memory Exercise

In a variation of the emotional memory exercise, you can have your partner look at the picture of a person, scene, or news story they have chosen. You can go through the same exercise, but have your partner focus on looking at this picture and allowing it to evoke any emotions that come up instead of reliving a memory. You can go through your immediate intuitive impressions and write them down, followed by intentionally switching your attention to conscious analysis of your partner's emotional state. As with the previous exercise, you can ask for feedback and compare notes with your partner at the end and ponder the results.

Comforting or Helping Someone in Crisis

We can tap into our intuition to create better communication with the people around us. When you find yourself in a situation that leaves you baffled, overwhelmed, confused, or downright clueless about what to say to a friend, relative, or coworker in crisis, simply ask your intuition for advice. When you know that you need to comfort that person or help them, but you don't know how, just tune in to your intuition and ask what would be the most healing words and actions for this person in the moment. You can also ask how to go about approaching them.

I suggest priming with the diamond light meditation, picturing your inner light shining and melting all the tension, discomfort, and fear away. Do this for a few cycles of breath. You can also imagine your friend in front of you. Observe their body language and the expression on their face, as well as their tone of voice or any other sensory impressions; notice how they seem stressed out or hurting and in need of something to comfort them. Ask your friend in your mind (or out loud if you have privacy): "What would you like to receive from me to feel better?" or "What can I do for you right now that will comfort you?"

If you do not receive an answer, try again by placing one hand on your heart to help you connect with your compassion for this person. When you ask your question, keep your intention of helping this person to heal.

Tension in a Relationship

When you're experiencing conflict or tension with someone, I suggest spending plenty of time priming, to assuage any worry or agitation. You may also wish to do the diamond light meditation, which can work to create a sense of protection around you, especially if you're concerned about remaining in your own essence due to the other person having a strong or overwhelming personality.

Imagine that person in front of you and ask: "What do I need to do and say now for our highest good, for both of us to heal?"

In general, before you speak to the other person, it can be good practice to check in with your intuition first, then your logic, just like looking at your rear and side mirrors while driving. Connect with your heart and gut, perhaps through your intuition gesture, and allow yourself to speak from these places, bringing both compassion and intuition into your communication.

Bill was intimidated by one of his key customers. He did not know what to do about this business relationship; he only knew that he wanted to keep it. We did some priming together, and I had him imagine this customer standing in front of him in a spacious place. Bill brought his attention to his heart and imagined turning a light on inside it in a color that symbolically represented empathy for him—in this case, yellow. I had him picture his customer as a small child for whom he could easily feel compassion. Then, I had Bill imagine the yellow light from his heart shining on this little kid and making him feel safe. Bill asked the child what he could do for him. The answer was to make him feel seen and appreciated. Bill asked how he could do this. The customer's answer was, "With a softer attitude and understanding." Bill realized that he had not invested enough time and effort into cultivating a connection with this customer as a person, so he decided then and there that he'd explore this.

You can ask your intuition: "What is a sincere thing this person wants to hear, and what can I say for both of our benefits?" If we all set the intention of kindness and consider the emotional state of others before we say or do anything, the world could be a better place. Before we do anything, we can ask, "What is one thing I can do for this person to help them?" When we are communicating, we are usually thinking of what we need to say instead of listening to the other person with all our attention and intuition. If we could instead tap into what the other person needs to hear in order to feel safe, connected, and in an overall good place, conflicts could be resolved more easily.

Intuition can help raise your awareness of the emotional landscape around you, which can increase empathy and improve relationships when combined with the intention of kindness in your words and actions. When you are about to react to someone else, tune in to your intuition and ask what their underlying emotions might be.

When you want to tap into your intuition with respect to people you are close to, it can be more challenging, especially for people you love, such as family or close friends, since what you know about them or want for them could interfere with this practice. Practicing tapping into your intuition in many different ways can prepare you for approaching conflict with loved ones, as well as genuinely attuning to what they truly need. Once you know your intuition well and have a good sense of how it feels and how it communicates with you, it becomes easier to distinguish between your wishes or conscious thoughts. You can double-prime yourself and use the various techniques in this book to remove your conscious mind and emotions from the picture.

The Essence of a Person

When checking in with your intuition about others, it isn't very productive to ask reductive questions like, "Is this a good or a bad person?" Good and bad are two extremes. There is a huge spectrum between them, and such judgments are subjective. For example, someone who is good to me may not be so good to you.

One question you can ask when you tune in to your intuition might be, "Can I be friends with this person?" Then, you can drill down deeper by asking a question like, "What is the essence of this person?" or "How can I make a connection with this person?"

When you are doing this kind of exercise, remember not to analyze their outer appearance. Our mind is very conditioned to do this, unfortunately. When we see someone young, we may assume they are single, still looking for their path in life, energetic, and many other qualities we associate with youth. When we see someone who appears older, our mind might conclude that they are retired, have children and grandchildren, and know what their life is all about. Such assessments may be completely inaccurate. When tapping into your intuition, you need to start with a blank slate. Especially when you're trying to gain intuitive insights about a person, you need to make sure that you are not coming to conclusions based on their age, gender, or any other quality that can be used to discriminate against someone. Every human being is a wealth of characteristics, desires, experiences, knowledge, and wisdom. We can never conclude that someone would be one way or another, based on a prejudiced assessment. Everyone is full of surprises, and that is part of the richness and fun of these intuitive exercises.

Private Garden Party

If you would like to gain some insight into your relationships with others in general, you can try this exercise. Settle in a comfortable quiet place and take a few deep breaths. Imagine comforting, warm light in a soothing color surrounding you. Allow this light to form into a ball that you can sit inside; imagine it lifting you up, so that you're floating in time and space, until you land in a beautiful garden.

Step into this garden and imagine feeling your feet on the ground. Bring in all the sensory details around you: the colors of the flowers and butterflies, the birdsong, the soothing qualities of a trickling fountain—anything you would like in this private garden that is all yours. Imagine walking around and touching leaves, tree trunks, and stones, enjoying their textures. Feel the temperature in the air and the gentle breeze.

Choose a place to sit in this garden and face the gate that allows you to enter the garden. Notice what the gate looks and feels like, and if there is a fence or hedge around your garden. Now, invite the people in your life to come and visit you in your garden. Imagine them entering through the gate. Notice their body language and if they come in readily or hesitate. Let them come and sit with you and have a conversation, or just pass through. Note how they act and what you choose to do.

When you feel you are done with this garden party, gently bring yourself back to your current physical environment. To do this, you can imagine stepping back into the ball of light, which lifts you up and brings you back. Feel the contact points of your seat or bed with your body. Move your arms, legs, fingers, and toes, remembering where you are physically as you slowly flutter your eyes open. Take a few minutes to write down your experiences so that you can go deeper into them the next time you try this meditation or after some other priming exercise. For example, if a family member or a friend chose to just stand by the gate and not enter the garden and sit and chat with you, you can choose to tune in to any blocks in your relationship.

Connection Between People

This exercise can help you gain insights into the relationship or connection between people. For example, you may be curious about how good the relationship is between your manager at work and their manager. This could impact your and your team's work and relationships with your manager, as well. After priming yourself, you can imagine these two people in a specific environment, such as an office or living room. How and where do they sit—close to or away from each other? What kind of nonverbal cues do you pick up from their body language? Can you imagine them turning toward each other and having a conversation while sitting in comfortable poses, or does one of them look tight or stressed out, perhaps with their arms crossed over their chest? What do their facial expressions seem to say?

You can go deeper into this exercise by imagining yourself in this place. How do you fit in, and where and how do you choose to sit? How do they respond to this? Do you have a comfortable conversation, or does anyone seem stressed or distant? Imagine asking one or both of them what their advice would be to reduce this tension. Ask your intuition directly what you can do and what your role could be in this connection. Thank your intuition for the answers and remember them as you gently come back to your physical environment.

Another way to practice tuning in to the connection or dynamics between people is similar to picking up character traits from pictures of people you don't know. You need a practice partner for this. Have your practice partner show you a picture of two or more people they know but whom you have never met and know nothing about. Look at the picture, letting your judgments and conscious analysis go and just observing their body language, facial expressions, how they sit or stand together, the space between them, and so on. Ask your intuition what the connection is between these people. You are not trying to get specific insights here, such as if they are mother and daughter. You are trying to feel the state of the relationship between them, including if they are close, if they seem to trust each other, if one makes more of the decisions in the relationship, and other such dynamics. Try to capture the first insights you get and trace them back to your root insight if you find yourself analyzing or consciously thinking about it. Share what you receive from your intuition with your practice partner and ask for their feedback.

I do this exercise with my students after we practice deciphering character traits of individuals from photos. They might pick up certain dynamics, such as one person being a teacher or mentor for the other, or tension in the relationship based on one or more of them holding grudges for a long time. Sometimes I combine tuning in to people on their own and their connections with others, using the same picture. I clip the picture of two or more people to show one person at a time and we go over the character traits my students pick up; then, I show them the full picture and ask how they feel about the connection and the dynamics between the people. What they pick up from individual close-ups can also aid them in tapping into the connection between people later on, as long as they look at the group picture after some priming. It's important for us to have a clean slate, so we don't make assumptions and perceive a pair or group of people with that bias. For example, if a person in the group seemed to be very wise, we should not look at the group dynamics with the assumption that everyone else goes to this person for advice, based only on what we picked up about that person intuitively. We still need to clear our mind, let go of judgments, and perceive the group as a whole to feel the dynamics that are present.

Checking on a Friend or Relative

Our intuition can give us clues on how to approach someone we're worried about. Jenny came to a session preoccupied about her friend Belinda, whom she had just talked to on the phone. Belinda had a stressful marriage, and Jenny was worried that her friend was sacrificing too much for her husband by moving far away from her own family and friends for him.

I had Jenny close her eyes and imagine being lifted in the air by a gentle cloud that took her to Belinda's house. Then, I had her imagine approaching the door, all while feeling her feet on the ground and noticing the visual details of the front yard and the house. Then, she rang the doorbell. Jenny told me that Belinda opened the door and looked well and happy. She invited Jenny in. I asked Jenny where she felt or saw Belinda's husband in this scene. All of this was for the purpose of helping Jenny sense Belinda's husband's role in all of this.

Jenny was surprised to see that Belinda's husband was not in this scene at all. We had her tune in to what she could ask or say to Belinda the next time they talked. Her intuition immediately brought in that she could ask what Belinda liked about her new place. This was the first time Jenny considered that her friend might have had her own reasons for moving and might have wanted a new start in life.

Revisiting Shared History

Jake wanted to understand the strain he had in his relationship with his older sister. They were very close as kids and played together all the time, although the age difference between them was five years. He felt that they had grown further and further apart since his sister's late teenage years. His logic said that this was because she was starting to feel like a grown-up and thinking about her future. He was still confused about why they did not become closer in their later years, when the age difference didn't matter anymore.

Jake tried to talk to her about this but did not get an enthusiastic response. We primed him with some deep breathing, followed by imagining that he was walking on a beautiful, quiet country road, which always relaxed him. I had him gently take himself back to their childhood years, starting around age five for him and ten for her. We let his imagination build the scenes as they played outdoors. Jake noticed that his sister was very protective of him and loved to take care of him, as if she were his second mom. He received the insight that this role was something she enjoyed and that fit her personality.

We took Jake on a journey through their different ages, having him just observe and not analyze their interactions. Jake realized that, as he became more and more independent, his sister grew confused about her role in their relationship and started to withdraw. We had him ask his intuition about a step he could take to build a deeper relationship with his sister. He received, "Just ask for her help with something." Jake realized that he hadn't done that in years—not only with his sister but also with other people in his life. When we discussed what he thought about this guidance from his intuition, he said that it made sense. He also felt it would help him grow and allow his sister and other people into his life to express care for him.

What's Your Role in My Life?

Sometimes it's difficult to tune in to the lesson in a relationship, as our emotions may keep flooding in when we focus on the other person. This could be because the relationship is loaded with expectations, disappointments, or emotional baggage. It might also be that we are very different from the other person. In such cases, it's possible to turn the tables and ask that person a question; then, have your intuition speak through them.

Claire had an academic advisor with whom she had a complicated relationship. She had a hard time tuning in to what she could do to improve this relationship or discern what she was supposed to learn from it. After doing some priming to calm her mind and emotions, we had her imagine sitting in neutral territory with her advisor, such as a coffee shop instead of the advisor's office, which could help to mitigate the power difference between them.

Claire used all her senses, imagining the sounds, smells, sights, and tactile sensations of this interaction. I had her ask her advisor what her role was in Claire's life, as well as what she could learn from and do about it. She received the insight that her relationship with her advisor was not balanced. Claire was always in pleasing mode, which made her play it safe and not go deep in her research. Her advisor explained that her role was to teach Claire to open her horizons and explore more deeply. Claire weighed this against what her logic was saying and decided to have a conversation with her advisor about new angles she could go into in her thesis.

Looking Deep into the Heart or Mind

Eva was having a hard time with a new friend at her college. She described her friend as being simultaneously needy and emotionally aloof, which was a confusing and disorienting combination. After priming, I had Eva imagine her friend standing in front of her. I asked her to focus on her friend's heart area and imagine a window or door there. Then, I had Eva look at or imagine the details of the window she saw, such as if it was open or closed, if there were curtains or shutters, if those were open or closed, and so on.

This served as extra priming, as well as symbolic representation denoting how open her friend was to sharing her emotions. Eva sensed that the window was partially open and asked her intuition what was in her friend's heart. She immediately got the response that there was insecurity and a craving for love. We let that sit in Eva's own heart space for a few moments, as she realized how similar this was to herself.

I had Eva look at her friend's forehead next and imagine a window or door there. Just as she'd done with the window in her friend's heart, she observed the details of the door she now saw. The door was old and closed but had a key in the lock. Eva symbolically asked for permission to unlock the door to get a sense of what was on her friend's mind. What she immediately received was her friend's need to prove herself, which also felt familiar.

After we gradually and gently brought Eva's attention back to her current physical environment and had her open her eyes, we discussed what she received from her intuition and how it felt. She had much more compassion for her new friend.

As I mentioned with respect to Bill's challenges with his customer, you can also use the method of imagining someone you're having difficulty with as a small child, which often enables us to expand our compassion and empathy for others. Just notice how old this person appears to be in your imagination. You might see that they're in a playground or at a school. Simply notice them. Let your conscious analysis and judgments go, and capture what your intuition brings forward. Perhaps you see them as happy, shy, or reflective. You can also follow the steps I used with Eva in the example above.

When I had Eva imagine her new friend as a little kid, the first impression her intuition picked up was that this child didn't receive enough love and truly craved it. As we discussed this later, Eva said this had given her a whole new perspective about her new friend, and more compassion and patience for her.

Hard to Get Through to Someone?

Have you been in a situation where you needed to communicate with someone but they were very hard to get through to? Ravi was puzzled by and somewhat worried about his business partner, Avinash, who was friendly and helpful but always seemed to have a wall up when it came to others getting too close.

After a priming exercise, I guided Ravi to imagine Avinash in an open field or space filled with light, with a fence or shield around him. I told Ravi to observe this fence or shield curiously; if any judgments came in or he started to consciously analyze, he could take a few deep breaths and let those judgments and analysis go. I asked what kind of fence or shield Avinash had around him. For example, was it a brick wall, or a hedge with bushes, or flowers, or light? How high was the fence? Were there gates or doors?

Ravi saw a brick wall that was about three feet tall, with a wooden door in it. I had him tune in to what this was telling him about how to approach Avinash in order to build a deeper connection. I even had Ravi ask the wall directly for this guidance. Ravi had the sense that Avinash was a private person but, in time, would open up with the people he trusted. His intuition was telling him to give Avinash time and space as they built trust.

The fence or shield you can sense around a person is a powerful metaphor that reveals information about how open they are and what their boundaries might be. As you learned in chapter 5, your intuition can absolutely speak loud and clear through metaphors and symbols. But when you try this technique, keep in mind that it's important to respect others' boundaries rather than pushing through them. Your focus should always be on intuitive guidance that can help you understand that person and allow for a more harmonious relationship.

Key Takeaways

- It's possible to hone our skill of noticing what's happening beyond the surface so that we can experience more harmonious relationships with other people, or at the very least, recognize what our intuition is telling us about them.
- Research has shown that people are able to decode nonverbal cues to gauge others' emotions, personalities, intentions, attitudes, or skill levels.
- It's important to remember that reading another person isn't a supernatural ability. We are built to be able to read nonverbal cues. We use this ability in our daily lives without even noticing.
- We can work with our intuition in everyday situations when coming across strangers or even people we know, by quickly tuning in to any impressions or insights we

receive about them.

- A wonderful way of working with intuition is by looking at photographs of someone you don't know and will likely never meet, then allowing your intuition to speak to you through this exploration. We can also use pictures of others to access our intuition about the emotions those people might have been feeling.

- Another great way to work with intuiting emotions is through asking another person to step into an especially powerful memory, which can elicit a strong (and strongly felt) emotional state. They'll do this without telling you what the memory is; then, you'll see what you can pick up about it.

- When you find yourself in a situation that leaves you baffled, overwhelmed, confused, or downright clueless about what to say to a friend, relative, or coworker in crisis, simply ask your intuition for advice.

- When you're experiencing conflict or tension with a friend, family member, colleague, or business associate, you can spend more time than usual priming to assuage any worry or agitation.

- To intuit the essence of a person, it's a good idea to avoid simplistic or all-or-nothing assessments. Every human being is a wealth of characteristics, desires, experiences, knowledge, and wisdom. We can never conclude that someone would be one way or another based on a prejudiced assessment.

- There are a number of methods presented in this chapter that you can use to gauge your sense of connection with the people in your life, which can give you insights into practical ways to approach your relationships.

- No matter how far away our loved ones are, we can always use our intuition to check in on them and to garner new realizations about them, as well as our mutual history, that we might not have previously considered.

- One of the deepest ways we can work with intuition on other people is by asking the simple question, "What is your role in my life?" This also helps us understand the ways someone else might be a force for our growth.

- The fence or shield that you might sense around a person is a powerful metaphor that reveals information about how open they are and what their boundaries might be. Working with this metaphor can give you insights into how to navigate your relationship with both respect and ease.

Reflections

- Were there any practices in this chapter that stood out as particularly intriguing or useful to you? Which ones would you like to practice further?

- Were there any exercises that you felt less drawn to? What made them less appealing?

- Identify at least three people in your life—acquaintances, friends, loved ones, or colleagues—you'd like to receive specific intuitive guidance on. Choose your favorite exercise and try using it with respect to these individuals. Write your insights in your journal and check these against your logic and advice from others who know these people well.

- Practice any of the exercises that might be helpful in allowing you to develop empathy and understanding for the people you want more intuitive guidance on. Often, when people desire to attune to their intuition for the purpose of stronger relationships, they might be unknowingly focused on getting the other person to change—or they might be focused on how they can benefit from the relationship. Instead, what if you were to focus on ways to be present for this other person and understand them from their own perspective? How does this change your relationship?

CHAPTER 8

Deeper Healing for the Soul—Intuition for Self-Care

Intuition is a powerful tool for self-care, especially when we find ourselves in periods of transition, grief, or depletion. Often, when life becomes overwhelming, our attention is directed outward—toward obligations, people, and responsibilities. We can easily lose touch with our inner needs and desires. In these times, intuitive practices offer us the ability to reconnect with ourselves, guiding us back to a place of inner balance and nourishment. By tuning in to our intuition, we can better understand what our body, mind, and spirit truly need in challenging moments, offering us a form of self-care that goes beyond just physical or mental health.

The beauty of intuition as a self-care tool is its ability to guide us without judgment, showing what feels healing and nurturing rather than what we think we should do. It creates space for us to listen to the subtle callings of our inner world— whether it's a craving for rest, a need to move, or a call to reach out for support. In times of depletion or grief, this inner voice becomes a sanctuary where we can find gentle guidance, allowing us to take care of ourselves in ways that might not be obvious through logic alone. Intuition combined with our conscious reasoning empowers us to make decisions based on what nourishes our souls rather than what drains us.

Self-care often requires us to honor our own rhythms and boundaries, and intuition is a guide in that process. It helps us distinguish between what is genuinely restorative and what might be a temporary distraction or an expectation placed on us by others. In periods of emotional or physical depletion, intuition acts as an ally, offering us the wisdom to slow down when necessary, to rest without guilt, and to give ourselves permission to heal at our own pace. By tuning in to our intuition, we honor the delicate balance of being human—acknowledging our pain and allowing our bodies and hearts the space to recover and renew.

Here, since I've been emphasizing the importance of checking your intuitive insights against your logical analysis, I want to say that self-care is not just an intuitive practice; it also invites us to engage our logical minds. Our logic can guide us toward nourishing actions, like choosing rest or taking time for ourselves—but often, logic may also push us to prioritize tasks, responsibilities, or the expectations of others—leading us away from the very self-care we need. In our "doing" society, we are conditioned to focus on productivity and achievement, which may cause us to ignore the subtle needs of our body, mind, and spirit. This is where intuition becomes an essential ally, guiding us to pause, listen, and honor what our deeper selves are asking for, whether it's rest, support, or simply space to grieve. What might you be ignoring in your body right now that could be a key message from your intuition waiting to guide you toward deeper self-care? Let's tune in and still weigh the guidance we receive against our logic; whenever it's possible to include, we can also complement our findings with research from experts in that specific area.

Body Scan for Checking in with Your Body

A body scan is a simple but powerful mindfulness practice that involves directing your attention to different areas of your body, noticing any sensations, and tuning in to your body's messages. It's often used in mindfulness-meditation training to cultivate awareness, but you don't need formal training to benefit from this version. The goal isn't to diagnose or analyze, but to become more attuned to how your body feels and what it might be telling you. This practice can serve as a tool for self-care, helping you connect with your body in a deeper way and cultivate an intuitive understanding of your physical and emotional state. It's a great way to check in with yourself, especially when you're feeling physically or emotionally low, and develop a deeper awareness of your body and emotions. It's an opportunity to listen to the subtle messages your body is sending, creating space for self-care and healing, and can also be used for priming when you have other questions for your intuition.

Start by finding a quiet, comfortable place where you can relax without distractions. Close your eyes, or soften your gaze, and take a few deep breaths, allowing your body to relax with each inhale and exhale. The goal is to let go of tension and clear your mind. Once you're settled, bring your attention to your feet. You can even imagine a small version of yourself walking and exploring there, if you like. Notice any sensations you might feel—warmth, tightness, tingling, or sometimes nothing at all. Ask your feet if they need anything from you and listen quietly for any intuitive responses. There's no need for judgment or analysis; just notice and be present with whatever you feel.

Once you've scanned your feet, thank them and gently shift your focus to your lower legs. Again, pay attention to any sensations you notice, and ask them what they might need. Continue this process as you move upward through your body: knees, thighs, hips, abdomen, chest, shoulders, arms, neck, and head. As you reach your abdomen, check in with your internal organs—especially any areas that might be calling your attention, like your stomach, liver, or heart. You don't have to scan every single part; just follow your intuition and focus on areas that feel significant.

When I guided Aditi through a body scan, she became aware of tension and discomfort in her shoulders. I asked her to bring her full attention to the sensations there, as if she were exploring her shoulders with curiosity. I had her place one hand on her shoulder, focusing entirely on the sensations of touch, and then repeat with the other shoulder. After a minute or two, I asked her to look at her shoulders in a mirror, bringing pure attention to them without any judgment or conscious analysis. To add a playful twist, I encouraged her to turn her head and move her shoulders toward her nose, paying attention to her sense of smell.

Once Aditi felt connected to her shoulders, we asked her intuition to speak through them. She wasn't sure how to express it at first, so I encouraged her to sit with the feeling and then journal about whatever came to her. She wrote, "What about Aditi?" The message was clear—she had been neglecting herself, focusing too much on taking care of others and not enough on her own needs. Her intuition gave her the answer: "Dance." Aditi had trained in the traditional dances of her native culture but hadn't made time for it recently. After our session, she decided to take a dance break before diving back into her busy day.

Partial Body Scan

If you're short on time or in a situation where you can't do a full body scan, you can still tap into your body's wisdom by focusing on just one or two areas that catch your attention. Maybe you feel drawn to your belly, your fingers, or your knees—whatever it is, let your focus land there. Tune in, listen quietly, and see what your body might be telling you. Sometimes, a simple check-in can reveal surprising insights or requests.

Take Olga, for example. She came to me with a heavy feeling in her heart, but no clear reason for it. I had her close her eyes and take a few deep breaths, focusing on the movement of her abdomen to ground herself. Then I asked her to bring her attention to her heart. Instead of asking, "What's wrong with you?" she phrased her question gently: "What can I do for you, heart?" That shift in language felt more nurturing to her, and her intuition answered: it was about love—giving and receiving it. Her heart told her that she needed to open up more.

Curious, we followed up with a second question: "Where can I start?" The answer was clear—Olga needed to find something that would put her in a flow state—something she loved so much that she'd lose herself in it. The answer came to her immediately: yoga. She realized that reconnecting with her yoga practice would help open her heart again.

This mini body scan isn't just about checking in with your body's sensations—it can also serve as a springboard for your intuition, helping you ask the right questions and receive powerful insights. It's a simple yet deeply revealing practice you can fit into any part of your day.

Partial Body Scan with Movement

If it's hard for you to focus on different parts of your body, or if you just want to shake things up a bit, try combining body awareness with movement. Moving your body can give your mind something else to focus on, which can help you tune in more easily. Here's an exercise you can do with your feet and legs, even while sitting—perfect if you're looking for a quick grounding practice. And if you're lying down or have other areas of your body in mind, feel free to adapt this for your own needs.

Start by sitting somewhere comfortable, take off your shoes or slippers, and place your feet flat on the floor or ground. Pay attention to how your feet feel against the surface beneath you. Press them down, then release. Roll your feet around, noticing the different sensations as they move. Let go of any distracting thoughts or judgments, and focus solely on your feet, feeling them connect to the ground beneath you.

Now, rock your feet back and forth, alternating between lifting them onto your toes, then your heels. Keep your awareness on the physical sensations of movement, letting your thoughts drift away. When you're ready, lift your right foot off the ground and gently rotate it at the ankle, bringing all your attention to that part of your body. Repeat for a few cycles of breath, then switch to your left foot.

Next, lift your right foot again, and gently sway your lower leg forward and backward. Focus on the sensations in your knee and the muscles surrounding it. After a few breaths, do the same with your left leg. As you move, feel yourself getting more connected to your body. When you're in the flow of the movement, drop a question or intention you have into your awareness and notice what comes up.

This exercise is a great way to calm your mind, especially if you tend to live more in your head than your body. It gives your busy thoughts a break and can help reduce stress. Plus, it primes you to receive intuitive insights. For those who love physical activity but don't always have time for it, this can be a great practice to get your energy flowing.

Victor spent most of his workday in back-to-back online and in-person meetings. As a rock climber, he craved movement but didn't always have the time or space for a full workout. He started doing this foot-movement exercise during meetings when he needed a bit of extra self-care or creativity to solve a problem. He even modified the way he moved his feet under the desk to mimic climbing steps, imagining his toes gripping the rocks in his favorite climbing spot. It was subtle enough for in-person meetings, but still effective for recharging and getting back to his creative flow.

Colors and Light Added to Body Scan

For a little extra fun, try imagining each body part in one or more colors. Picture them glowing with light, like each organ or body part is lighting up in its own special hue. As you focus on each part, tune in to its color and imagine that light shining brighter, helping you connect more deeply with it. You can ask your intuition what these colors might mean or what that body part might need. Maybe your stomach will say, "More veggies, please!" or your feet might ask, "How about some new walking shoes?" Stay curious and playful—think of it like you're chatting with your body, and let your intuition come alive.

Golden Leaves Meditation

This meditation is a gentle and relaxing exercise that can help you take time for yourself. During this meditation, you'll ask for a healing message to help you feel better in any kind of stressful situation, or even as a form of preventive care if you anticipate facing a challenge.

Find a quiet, comfortable spot where you can fully relax. Close your eyes or soften your gaze, and take a few deep, calming breaths, letting each exhale release the tension from your shoulders, neck, arms, legs, torso, and your entire body. Picture yourself being gently lifted by a soft breeze or a fluffy cloud rising effortlessly into the sky, and gliding toward a vast, lush green field. The air is fresh, and the land undulates in gentle hills.

As you walk through this peaceful landscape, you spot a magnificent tree perched atop one of the hills, its branches reaching toward the sky like welcoming arms. You make your way up to it. Find a cozy spot, sit down on the soft earth or on a nearby bench, your back resting against the solid trunk. Feel its deep support, as if the tree is wrapping you in a warm, protective embrace.

Golden leaves begin to fall from the tree—not the dry, brittle leaves of autumn, but vibrant, living leaves that glow with a soft, radiant light. As each leaf drifts down and lands gently on you, it infuses your body with soothing, healing energy. The golden light flows through you, calming your muscles, easing tension, and bringing a deep sense of relaxation that moves through your entire being, even grounding you through the soles of your feet. With every falling leaf, you release discomfort or stress, letting it flow away and dissolve into the earth beneath you.

Now, bring your hands together, palms upward, and feel a large, vibrant green leaf land softly in your hands. As you turn it over, you discover a healing message inscribed on its back, or perhaps you hear it whisper to you, or feel its meaning stir in your heart. Take a moment to absorb the message, thanking the leaf and the tree for their wisdom. Soon, a much larger leaf gently drapes over your back, like a soft, cozy blanket, continuing to soothe and heal you with each deep, steady breath.

When you're ready, feel the large leaf gently lift you up, guiding you back to your present environment. Notice where you are sitting—whether on a chair, the floor, or the earth—and gently begin to move your fingers and toes, stretch your body, and yawn, as if waking from a peaceful rest. Slowly open your eyes. Take a few quiet moments to reflect on your experience or jot down the intuitive messages you received in your journal.

I often guide my students and clients through this meditation, and many report receiving gentle, actionable advice, like taking a bubble bath or going for a walk in nature. Others receive deeper, life-affirming guidance, such as a reminder that "Everything will be OK in the end, and if it's not OK, it's not the end."

Bright Star Meditation

This meditation is a powerful tool for when you're feeling down or overwhelmed, especially when you need a reminder of your unique strength and essence. It serves as a gentle nudge to help you reconnect with your inner light and find the courage to keep going, no matter the challenges you face in your roles as a parent, sibling, friend, colleague, manager, and the like. Essentially, this meditation helps you to connect with your essence beyond all these roles.

Start by finding a quiet, comfortable place where you can sit or lie down. Close your eyes or soften your gaze, and take a few deep, slow breaths. With each exhale, imagine releasing any tension from your body, letting it melt away. Place your hand gently over your heart and envision a radiant star glowing under your palm. Picture this star in any color you like—maybe a brilliant gold, shimmering silver, pure white, or even a rainbow of changing colors, like a string of Christmas lights. This is your star. You are this star. Feel its warmth and brilliance growing within you as you focus on it, expanding in size and radiance. Let it grow until it surrounds you, filling the space around you with its comforting glow. You are sitting within your own shining light. Let yourself be comforted and warmed.

Take a moment to ask your intuition what you need right now to nurture yourself, heal, and find the peace, rest, and compassion you truly deserve. If you notice your mind wandering into thoughts, judgments, or analysis, gently dissolve these distractions by breathing deeply into the light of your star. With each breath, feel your mind quieting, letting go of any internal and external noise. When you're ready, ask your intuition once more what you need. Receive the answers that come and set the intention that you will remember them. Afterward, slowly bring your awareness back to your physical surroundings. Stretch, move, and yawn, as if waking up from a peaceful nap, and then open your eyes gently. Take a few moments to reflect on the messages you received, either by journaling or sitting quietly in contemplation. As always, run the intuitive guidance you received through your logic before following it.

One of my clients, a busy executive and mother of two young children, uses this meditation every morning before diving into her hectic day. She often receives what she calls "brilliant responses" from her intuition, helping her set a calm, confident tone for the day ahead. Even on her busiest days, she can quickly tap back into this sense of inner strength by imagining her star glowing brightly once more, refreshing her energy and focus.

Self-Care During Times of Grief

Grief is one of the most complex and layered emotions we can experience. It's not just sadness; it's a mix of love for what we've lost, longing to have it back; and sometimes frustration, anger, or disappointment at the painful reality that our life may never be the same again. Grief doesn't only come when we lose loved ones. We may grieve a place we can no longer visit, a chapter of our life that has closed, or even a part of ourselves—like our health after a life-altering illness. Some of us may grieve a job, a home, or a lifestyle that is now gone. Whatever form your grief takes, it's crucial to be kind and patient with yourself during this time. Grief can cloud your thoughts, making it hard to know what you need or how to care for yourself. This is where your intuition can be a guiding light.

Especially when grief feels overwhelming, it can be hard to think clearly. Take a moment to breathe deeply or engage in any gentle exercise that calms your mind. You might be surprised at what your intuition suggests when you ask, "What can I do for myself right now?"

One tool I turn to in times like these is the body scan I introduced earlier in the chapter. It helps me reconnect with my body, reminding me that I'm still here, still living, even in the midst of loss. After the recent passing of a very dear family member, I used this exercise to check in with myself. As I moved through my body, I felt a weight in my stomach, like a stone pressing down, a place where grief was settling. My intuition gently guided me to recall a soup recipe this family member had made for me, a comfort food that always made me feel loved. At first, my conscious mind hesitated, wondering if it would be too sad to eat it now. But my intuition whispered that it would be healing. So, I made the soup, stirring it slowly and allowing myself to feel the warmth and comfort of the memories. Each spoonful brought not just nourishment, but peace, as I remembered all the times we'd shared around the dinner table. In those moments, the grief softened, and I felt held by the love we had shared.

Cooking with Intuition

Lately, there's been a lot of buzz around intuitive eating, and while we may still be waiting for more research to fully understand its impact on our health, there's something simple and nourishing you can try right now: intuitive cooking. You don't need to be a chef or have a perfect recipe—just listen to what your body and the ingredients are telling you. Start by doing a body scan, tuning in to your energy, and any sensations in your body. Then, head to the grocery store or open your fridge, and let your intuition guide you to the healthy ingredients that feel right for you today.

Imagine that each vegetable, fruit, or herb is like a little personality waiting to be discovered. Take a moment to really connect with them the way we learned to connect with objects in chapter 6: Hold a head of lettuce, feel its texture, smell its freshness, and let go of any judgment. Ask it what it wants to be paired with and let that gentle pull guide you to another vegetable or ingredient that complements it. It's like you're creating a mini collaboration between you and your ingredients.

Once you start cooking, keep the connection going. Focus on the tactile sensations of chopping, the sound of the knife on the cutting board, and the way the aromas fill the air. Notice the beautiful colors of your ingredients as they come together in harmony. Ask them what spices they'd like to play with, and what will bring out their best flavors. In a way, your dish is throwing a little party; each ingredient brings its own unique flavor, and together, they nourish not just your body but your spirit too. Intuitive cooking isn't just about making food; it's about creating an everyday experience that's nourishing on every level as you tune in and let your senses guide you.

Key Takeaways

- Intuition is a powerful self-care tool that helps us reconnect with our inner needs during times of transition, grief, or depletion, guiding us toward healing and balance with gentle, judgment-free guidance.
- A body scan is a simple mindfulness practice that helps you connect with your body's sensations, tune in to its messages, and cultivate intuitive self-care, especially during times of physical or emotional depletion.
- Even when your time is limited, focusing on just one or two areas of your body can tap into your intuition, offering valuable insights and guidance.
- Combining body awareness with simple movement, like a seated foot exercise, helps ground your mind, reduce stress, and prime you for intuitive insights—perfect for moments when you need a quick recharge.
- Add a playful twist to body awareness by imagining each body part glowing in its own color, then tune in to what your intuition might reveal about what that part needs, like a fun, colorful conversation with your body.
- The golden leaves meditation is another technique that can help you release stress and connect with your intuition for guidance, whether you're facing a challenge or simply seeking preventive care.

- The bright star practice helps you reconnect with your inner light and strength, reminding you of your essence beyond any roles you play and offering guidance to nurture and heal yourself during overwhelming times.
- Grief is a complex emotion that blends love, loss, and longing, and during such times, tuning in to your intuition—whether through practices like body scanning or simply asking "What can I do for myself right now?"— can offer gentle guidance and comfort.
- Intuitive cooking involves connecting with your ingredients through your senses and body, letting them guide you to create nourishing meals that support both physical and emotional well-being.

Reflections

- What might you be ignoring in your body right now that could be a key message from your intuition waiting to guide you toward deeper self-care?
- When was the last time you paused in the middle of your grief to ask yourself, "What do I need right now?" What would happen if you tried?
- How can you differentiate between what your body truly needs and what you feel you should be doing in moments of emotional depletion?
- What if listening to the subtle cues of your intuition during a moment of overwhelm could transform your experience of grief or depletion? What might it lead you to do or create?

- In times when you feel emotionally or physically low, how could intuitive practices like body scans or mindful movement shift your energy and help you reconnect with a sense of peace or clarity?

CHAPTER 9

Master Your Intuitive Edge—Empower Your Practice with Further Techniques

Congratulations on reaching this milestone! You've made incredible progress on your journey to deepen your connection with your intuition. Whether it was your inner wisdom that led you here or curiosity from your mind, you've likely discovered just how much your intuition is already guiding you in your life. As you moved through the previous chapters, I hope you uncovered new ways to invite this powerful force into your daily experience, enriching everything in your life with more wonder and insight.

When we open ourselves to our intuition, it's as if the world becomes more vibrant—like discovering a new color or hearing a new note that was always there, waiting to be noticed. Intuition is a deeply personal gift, yet it's universal. It speaks uniquely to each of us, and as we've explored, its language varies from person to person. How it communicates with you may be different from others, and how you prime yourself for it is just as individual.

The tips and tools in this book are meant to inspire and guide you, but ultimately, this journey is about discovering your own unique ways of tapping into your inner wisdom. Now that you've absorbed the basics (or refreshed what you already knew), I encourage you to adapt the exercises to your own life and even create new ways to connect with your intuition.

This chapter offers playful ideas and further techniques to help you dive even deeper into the process so you can continue to explore and expand your connection with your inner guide. The possibilities are endless, and the more you experiment, the more you'll discover how your intuition is an invaluable ally on your path forward.

Visit a Wise Friend (or Yourself) at Any Age

Ready for a playful, intuitive adventure? Find a cozy spot to sit or lie down, take a few deep cleansing breaths, and relax into the moment. Now, imagine you're about to meet a very wise friend—someone who could be your age, older, or even younger; someone you know or perhaps do not. Choose a place for your meeting that sparks joy and creativity—maybe a peaceful home, a sunny park, or a lively public space. The more details you add, the better. Perhaps you arrive floating on a cloud or flying on the back of a giant bird—whatever feels fun and primes your whole being for this exercise.

Once you've arrived, tune in to your surroundings. What do you see, hear, and feel? Pay attention to the colors, textures, and sounds in the environment. As you approach your wise friend, take a moment to imagine what they look like and feel the excitement of meeting them. Now, sit down and have a heart-to-heart conversation. Ask any questions you have and allow your intuition to speak through your friend. Set the intention to capture and remember their answers.

Once your conversation is over, thank your wise friend. You can also consider a variation of this exercise. Instead of your friend, try visiting your younger or older self, depending on the guidance you need. Want a burst of creative energy? Check in with your younger self. Need wisdom and life experience? Your older self is there for that.

For an even more whimsical twist, imagine time-traveling to your future home or sacred space, where you discover little notes from your future self offering wisdom and advice. This adds an extra layer of fun and insight to your practice. I worked with a student, Shawn, who visited her sacred space and found an old wooden box containing a letter from her future self. The letter offered powerful solutions to her dilemma with her aging mother, and after reading it, she felt a deep sense of release and clarity.

When you're ready, gently bring yourself back to the present moment. Feel where you're sitting or lying down, move your fingers and toes, and flutter your eyes open. Take a moment to jot down the insights your wise friend—or younger or older self—shared. Compare these intuitive messages to what your conscious mind thinks and run them through your logical lens. You might be surprised by the wisdom you uncover, and it's a wonderful way to keep practicing and deepening your connection with your intuition.

So, go ahead—get creative, time travel, and let your intuition surprise you with its playful insights.

Use What You Love

Zelda, who had a passion for trains and traveling, came to me seeking clarity about her complicated teenage years. She was a restless soul with a strained relationship with her parents. To help her explore these emotions, I guided her through a visualization journey to visit her younger self. To make it fun and relaxing, we imagined a beautiful train station and a train that would take her back to those years. When the train arrived at her destination, we immersed her in the sensory details—the sights, sounds, and even the smells—to truly ground her in the scene.

Zelda found her younger self sitting under a large tree in the backyard, a book resting on her lap. I invited her to ask her younger self what she was yearning for, what expectations she had for herself, and what hopes she had for the future. As she observed, she noticed a sense of forced self-confidence and asked her younger self about it. Through this experience, Zelda received profound insights into her questions, which we later discussed. This exercise, which also takes a little from the technique of visiting your younger self, demonstrates how you can use familiar things or places you love to prime yourself for deeper exploration.

Another client, Grace, came to a session feeling overwhelmed by a mix of emotions, sadness being the most dominant. Since she loved cats, I guided her to imagine visiting an animal rescue center. I asked her to explore the space and choose a cat that represented her sadness. She found a yellow one that she decided to name Tangerine. When I asked what she'd like to do with Tangerine, she said she wanted to bring it to her home. As they cuddled and played in her living room, the cat became more lively. I suggested we shift the energy and have her ask Tangerine any questions it might have answers to. When she asked, "Why are you sad?" the cat replied with "loneliness."

I encouraged Grace to ask what they could do about it, and the answer was, "Go out more so you can make new friends." They spent time playing at a cat café, and soon other people and cats joined them. Grace wanted to continue, so we moved on to explore her anger. She found another cat that represented this emotion, and through a similar process, she gained insights into what lay beneath her anger and how she could address it.

By the end of the session, as Grace brought her attention back to her physical surroundings and opened her eyes, she felt refreshed and gained a deeper understanding of her emotions. As Grace also learned, we can anchor in what we love; this can then become a guide through our emotional landscapes so that we might experience greater clarity.

Insights into the Future

Intuition can be a powerful tool for gaining insight into situations you might face in the future. This isn't about fortune telling or knowing exactly what will happen, but rather using your nonconscious mind to uncover perspectives that can inform your conscious thoughts. When you're uncertain about how to approach a future situation, your intuition can help guide you by offering subtle insights that you might not have considered.

Take the case of Clarissa, who was uncertain about how to navigate a trip with a new friend. They were going to share expenses, but Clarissa wasn't sure how to approach the financial details. She had already spent time thinking about it and asked for advice from a few trusted people, but she continued to feel unsure. I guided her through a simple process: She closed her eyes, took deep breaths, and imagined a calming light surrounding her. With each inhale, she visualized the light filling her body, and with each exhale, she released any tension or discomfort. This kind of priming works well for her, but depending on the person, I might suggest a different approach—such as focusing on body sensations, like pressing your feet firmly into the ground or tracing your fingers along your arm to anchor your attention.

Once Clarissa felt centered, she imagined her trip in detail—considering the sights, sounds, and sensations she would encounter. As she let the scenario unfold without judgment or overthinking, she gained valuable insight about herself. She realized that she often hesitated to set clear boundaries and saw this trip as an opportunity to practice asking for what she needed, both before and during the trip. After the trip, Clarissa reported having a positive experience. She and her friend acknowledged their different needs and expectations, and by setting clear boundaries, they were able to enjoy the trip while still maintaining their independence.

This process demonstrates how intuition can offer subtle yet powerful guidance. By taking time to tune in, you may find that your intuition helps you gain clarity and perspective on a situation, leading to more informed and thoughtful decisions.

Intuition on Timing and Obstacles

Our intuition can offer remarkable insights into when we might achieve our goals, drawing on past experiences, knowledge, and observations of similar situations. We often do this effortlessly in everyday life—estimating how long it'll take to cook dinner, finish painting a room, run errands, or complete a task at work. We even account for possible setbacks without realizing it. For bigger dreams or projects, tapping into intuition can feel more challenging, but it's a rewarding and creative process when paired with conscious analysis.

Mateo dreamed of opening a gym café but saw it as a long-term goal. With family responsibilities, including ensuring his children's education, he felt he couldn't take the risks needed to pursue his passion just yet. Still, he wanted to keep his dream alive and gain a sense of when it might come to fruition. To help, I guided him through a visualization exercise.

I asked Mateo to imagine a miniature version of his gym café, place it inside an imaginary box, and watch the box move away from him, like rewinding a movie along a timeline marked with days, months, and years. When the box stopped, I had him pause, take a few deep breaths, and let his intuition speak. Instantly, he felt "five years" was the answer.

Next, I guided him to imagine the path to the box. Was it straight or winding? Were there hills, walls, or rocks—symbols of obstacles? As he observed, Mateo's intuition identified what these challenges represented and what he might need to do to overcome them. Whenever he started overanalyzing or saying things like "I think," I reminded him to pause, breathe, and reconnect with his intuition.

Through this process, Mateo gained not only a potential timeline for his dream but also valuable insights into how to navigate the obstacles in his path. It was a powerful reminder of how intuition, paired with a little creativity and logic, can help illuminate the way forward.

Taking Dictation from Your Intuition

Automatic writing is a process where you allow your hand to write freely without conscious control, letting your intuition guide the words and symbols that appear on the page. It's a powerful practice for unlocking emotions and connecting deeply with your inner wisdom.

To begin, try a priming exercise, such as meditation, a walk, or listening to music to clear your mind. Then, find a comfortable spot with your journal or a blank sheet of paper and a pen. While you can use a computer or phone, the tactile feeling of pen on paper often helps you sink deeper into the process.

Once you're ready, ask your intuition to share any messages it has for you, setting the intention to receive them through your writing. Let the words flow onto the page, and if any shapes, symbols, or drawings come to mind, feel free to include them. If you find it difficult to begin, use a prompt such as, "I would like you to know that . . ." or "My intuition would like me to know that . . ." and let your hand continue from there.

You can choose to make automatic writing a regular habit. Many of my clients who like to write enjoy doing it every day, but even once a week can bring powerful insights. Set aside five to ten minutes for each session, and try tying it to an existing routine, like writing just before bed or as soon as you wake up.

Stay open and unattached to forming regular sentences. Just be with the flow. You may get just one word, or a shape or symbol that you can go into in greater depth using the techniques in this book. With regular practice, automatic writing can become a therapeutic tool for emotional release and a clear channel for your inner guidance.

Put It on Stage

David came to a session feeling frustrated with his friends. He'd recently hung out with them but didn't enjoy himself and couldn't quite figure out why. He had tried thinking it through, but that only made him more frustrated. So, I guided him through an intuitive exercise to help him gain clarity in a creative and surprising way.

I asked David to close his eyes and take a few deep breaths to center himself. Then, I invited him to imagine a soft breeze picking him up and carrying him across time and space, gently setting him down in an empty theater. He took a seat in the audience, the perfect spot to observe. On stage, his friends began to appear, one by one or in groups—however his intuition placed them. He decided who stood where and adjusted the stage lights to spotlight each person or group, choosing their brightness and colors.

One small group glowed the brightest in David's imaginary theater, and I asked him to step onto the stage to join them. He naturally gravitated to the middle of the group but noticed his own spotlight was dim. This reflected how he often avoided drawing attention to himself—a powerful insight from his intuition.

I encouraged him to explore further. "What happens if you step closer to one of the other groups?" He tried but admitted it felt uncomfortable. "What makes it uncomfortable?" I asked. "I'd feel like I'm taking sides," he said. From there, we followed his feelings step-by-step, peeling back the layers of what taking sides meant to him and how it felt to stand apart.

If David began to overthink, I brought him back to the sensory details of the scene—how the curtains looked, the texture of the seats, or the way the stage lights illuminated the room. This grounded him in the moment, allowing his intuition to lead rather than his logical mind.

When the exploration felt complete, I guided him back. The same soft breeze gently returned him to the present moment. He reconnected with his physical surroundings, moving his fingers and toes, and slowly opened his eyes.

As we discussed his experience, David realized something profound: His need to avoid conflict often led him to hold back, even when it drained him emotionally. This insight gave him the clarity to address his frustration with his friends in a healthier way.

You can try this imaginative stage exercise yourself when you're seeking intuitive guidance about a situation or people in your life. Envision a theater where you can observe events or dynamics unfold from a distance. Watch from the audience, or step onto the stage to explore interactions and ask your intuition the questions on your mind. By creating this imaginary space, you separate yourself from the mental loops of overthinking and gain a fresh perspective rooted in intuition.

Put It in a Dark Room

This technique is similar to the previous one, but it's more like staging a play where the situation and people you're tuning in to become the setup and the characters on set. After priming yourself to relax and clear your mind, you create an imaginary scene—a dark room, quiet and full of potential, waiting for the spotlight to reveal what's hidden.

Adam was considering a new business partnership with two people he'd recently met. He had done all his home-work—researching the opportunity, analyzing the financials, and weighing the pros and cons. Still, he felt the need to check in with his intuition before making a final decision.

After a quick priming exercise, I asked Adam to close his eyes and imagine everyone involved in this deal gathering in a dimly lit room, much like actors getting into position before the start of a play. The setting he chose was an office—silent, shadowy, and still. Then, in his mind's eye, he turned on the lights.

As the imaginary scene came to life, Adam watched each person closely. He tuned in to their presence, the energy in the room, and his own feelings as he observed them. After a moment, he stepped into the scene himself. He noticed how the atmosphere shifted, how they reacted to his arrival, and how it all felt on a gut level. The result? A sense of unease. His intuition sent a clear signal that something about this partner-ship didn't sit right. While he didn't dismiss the deal entirely, he realized he needed to tread carefully moving forward.

By stepping into an intuitive scene like this, you give your-self the space to sense the deeper dynamics of a situation. It's like flipping the lights on in a room you didn't realize was full of insights just waiting to be revealed.

One Thing at a Time

Jessica has always been deeply connected to music. During one of our sessions, we used one of her favorite pieces, Vivaldi's "Four Seasons," to help her tap in to her intuition. As the music played, she would often lose herself in the flow, her mind and emotions quieting into stillness. But she was also worried about her sister, who was facing financial struggles, and intrusive thoughts about this kept surfacing.

To help her focus, I suggested she tune in to just one set of instruments, like the cellos, and intentionally tune out the others. This level of focus demanded so much attention that it left little room for her worries to creep in. Knowing Jessica loves visualizations, I had her imagine the orchestra on a stage, bringing the cellos forward while gently pushing the other instruments into the background. She loved this approach, saying it made it much easier to concentrate on the cellos, allowing her to stay present and free from rumination.

Jessica's creative mind lit up. She asked if this tech-nique—mentally bringing something into focus and pushing distractions into the background—could work for other prac-tices, like tuning in to someone in a group. She imagined drawing that person closer in her mind's eye while letting the others fade back.

It was a brilliant idea, and it reminded me of a technique filmmakers often use: When they want the audience to focus on a specific detail, like an actor's face or an old clock, they zoom in or blur the background. I shared this analogy with Jessica, and she decided to try it during a group dinner. She practiced zooming in on her sister with visualization and intentional attention while letting the rest of the room fade into the background. Later, she excitedly told me how well it had worked. This simple yet powerful technique helped her sharpen her focus and tune in to her sister's emotional and mental state with ease.

Pick Your Place

Naomi is a talented artist who wanted to connect with her intuition to discover the next steps in her creative journey. I asked her a simple question: "If you could go anywhere in the world to develop your art and find inspiration, where would it be?" Without hesitation, she said, "Italy."

To help her tap into her intuition, we embarked on an imaginary trip to Italy. I guided her to dive deeply into the experience by focusing on each sense, one at a time. She imagined the stunning visual details—the intricate architecture, vibrant art, and golden light of the Italian countryside. She tuned in to the sounds of bustling piazzas and distant church bells, the aroma of fresh paint and Italian cuisine, and even the textures of ancient stone walls and cool marble floors.

In her mind, she explored an ancient art school, envisioning herself walking through its hallways, attending a class, and soaking in the creative atmosphere of the town around her. As she let go of conscious thoughts and obstacles, she delighted in the freedom of imagining without limits.

Once she was fully immersed, I encouraged her to ask her intuition what her next steps could be. When we gently brought her back to the present, her ideas were flowing effortlessly. She was in the zone, inspired and clear-headed. We explored the ideas together, discussing which ones felt most actionable and meaningful to her.

You can try this technique as well. Imagine yourself in a place that inspires you—a destination where your creativity and intuition can thrive. Engage your senses to bring the scene vividly to life. Once you're fully immersed, ask your intuition for guidance on your next steps. When you're ready, gently return to the present by feeling your physical surroundings— become aware of your body, stretch, and slowly open your eyes. Finally, take the insights you've gained and run them through the filter of your logic before making big decisions or taking action. This blend of imagination, intuition, and practicality can lead to truly transformative ideas.

Deeper into the Words

Sometimes, your intuition speaks in whispers—with just a single word. I've experienced this often during intuition or life-coaching sessions. As a client begins talking about their situation, a word will suddenly pop into my mind. When this happens, I usually ask for permission to share it and then invite the client to explore what it might mean to them.

One powerful way to deepen this exploration is by twirling the word in the mind, without consciously analyzing. For clients who enjoy visualizing, I suggest imagining the word written in the air, with the letters playfully floating around. In one session, the word sustenance surfaced for a client. As she visualized the letters dancing in the air, other words emerged—love, nurturing, and care. She tuned in to these words one by one, letting them guide her to a deeper understanding of what her intuition was revealing.

In another session, a client repeatedly encountered the word struggle. When we had her twirl it around in her mind and imagine the letters floating freely, something magical happened. The letters seemed to rearrange themselves, and an extra one appeared, forming the phrase tug less. For her, this was a clear message: She needed to let go of micromanaging her team and allow things to unfold naturally, creating ease and flow instead of resistance.

You can try this technique too. If a word has been lingering in your mind or puzzling you, let it float playfully in your imagination. See if the letters rearrange, reveal hidden meanings, or connect you to other ideas. Farouk used this approach when tuning in to his feelings about a frustrating situation with his friend Ahmed. During the exercise, he imagined the words he associated with Ahmed swirling in the air between them. As he looked behind and beneath the words, deeper meanings surfaced—care, history, and support. These words reminded him of their true connection and inspired him to reach out, mending their friendship.

Another playful way to engage with words is by singing them. Whether you hum a familiar tune or make up a melody on the spot, singing allows you to connect with the word in a lighthearted, intuitive way. By singing without strain, you open yourself to creative insights. Often, ideas or clarity will emerge spontaneously, either in the moment or shortly after.

So, the next time a word pops into your mind, let it guide you. Visualize it, play with it, or sing it—and see where your intuition leads you.

Intuition for Complex Problems

Many of the exercises in this book have focused on what I like to call *fast intuition*. We experience this when we capture the first response we receive from our intuition after priming. Often, this can give us good results, as fast intuition works well in situations where conditions are similar to what we might have previously experienced. In other cases, where we don't have much prior knowledge about the situation or when we need to come up with new ways of doing things under new conditions or in totally new areas, *slow intuition* is a better approach. Slow intuition is the result of musing and mulling over things in a relaxed way over time. We can sleep on it, daydream about it, or take it out for a walk, then wait and see what our intuition comes up with while we rest our conscious problem-solving mind.

Sometimes, when I am coaching a client and the conversation and direction seem stuck, we take a break and a few deep breaths to tune in to our intuition; we usually get an image, a vision, a word, or some other hunch to be able to untie the knot and move forward.

Intuition often emerges when you are relaxed and not actively focused on a problem. Scientists, including Nobel Prize winners and artists, frequently report sudden insights into complex problems they've worked on for years, as detailed in Guy Claxton's book *Hare Brain, Tortoise Mind*. Often, they cannot explain how these insights arise, which likely stems from their intuition—a result of accumulated experiences combined with rapid, efficient evaluation of possible solutions. In his 1994 book *Descartes' Error: Emotion, Reason, and the Human Brain*, Antonio Damasio explains that decision-making often involves both analytical reasoning and intuition. While we can consciously think through relevant factors, intuition handles the complex calculations of outcomes and trade-offs, leveraging unconscious processes.

Kenneth Gilhooly of the University of Hertfordshire explored this further in his 2016 *Frontiers in Psychology* paper, "Incubation and Intuition in Creative Problem Solving." Reviewing cognitive-science research, he highlights how breaks from consciously working on a problem, known as incubation periods, can lead to intuitive insights. These unconscious processes, referred to as *unconscious work*, are particularly effective under the immediate incubation paradigm. In immediate incubation, a problem is introduced, and attention is quickly diverted to another task before participants fully engage with it. This approach enhances intuitive breakthroughs. In contrast, delayed incubation involves deeply engaging with the problem first, followed by a break. While both methods benefit from unconscious processing, immediate incubation appears to yield stronger results for creative problem-solving.

Taking a break can be one of the most powerful tools for solving difficult problems, especially those requiring fresh, creative thinking. Think back to a time when you were stuck on a crossword puzzle clue, gave up, and later—perhaps during an evening walk—the solution suddenly popped into your mind. We all know the value of giving our minds a rest but putting it into practice can be tricky.

Too often, we obsess over finding a solution, refusing to take a break until we've reached a certain point. Even when we do step away, we often ruminate on the problem, preventing our minds from truly resting. However, science backs up the benefits of giving our brains proper downtime. Cognitive studies show that when we set aside a problem and fully disengage from it—like in the incubation periods discussed earlier—our unconscious mind gets to work. This work can generate new ideas, which often emerge as a sudden aha moment during the break or when we revisit the problem. These intuitive leaps happen without a step-by-step chain of reasoning, the hallmark of true intuition.

This leads me to my take on the immediate incubation paradigm, which might remind you of the popular Pomodoro Technique. Created by Francesco Cirillo in the late 1980s, the Pomodoro Technique involves twenty-five minutes of focused work followed by a five-minute break. Its popularity has surged, especially as more people work from home. Inspired by the Pomodoro method—and the playful connection between incubation (like eggs) and the tomato-shaped timers used in the technique—I call my version *menemen*, after the delicious Turkish scrambled egg and tomato dish. You might already be practicing something similar without realizing it.

To do this exercise, consider a problem that you have been trying to solve for a while and don't have an answer to yet.

This can be about a work or home project, or something about your interactions with someone in your life—perhaps a family member, colleague, or friend.

1. Introduction: Take a quick look at the problem and mentally review all the solution options that you've previously considered. (Using the scrambled eggs and tomatoes metaphor, this is when you gather your ingredients, but you don't chop or crack anything just yet.)

2. Immediate Incubation/Unconscious Work: Prime yourself for unconscious problem-solving exactly the same way you would prime yourself for intuition. Go for a walk in nature, meditate, listen to relaxing music, mindlessly play your favorite computer game, lie down and stare at the ceiling or the sky—do whatever quiets down your mind and gives it a good break while calming your emotional state. (Going back to our delicious dish, this is when you warm the pan and melt the butter. Let your thoughts and worries melt away with a relaxing or fun activity.)

3. Conscious Work: Return to the problem and work on it for some time to come up with new solution options. Follow through with them. The fruits of unconscious work during the incubation period may rise up to your awareness as new ideas during this period. How much time you give to this step depends on the complexity of your problem, availability of your time, and your attention span. You can continue until you come to a natural stopping point when you feel stuck. (This step

is like cracking open the eggs, chopping the tomatoes, and pouring them into the pan and mixing them. You may be inspired to add spices you've never tried before, as the "priming" period has warmed up your intuition.)

4. Alternate Conscious and Unconscious Work: Alternate unconscious work (incubation) and conscious work (direct problem-solving) periods until you make sufficient progress for the day. If the problem is not solved that day, start with step 1 again the next day. (In our scrambled eggs with tomatoes metaphor, this would be stirring the mix until the scramble is cooked.)

You can alternate focused thinking with relaxation in whatever ratio feels doable and good to you, and appropriate for the problem at hand. You can try twenty-five minutes of conscious thinking and five minutes of floating in the primed state, or one hour of thinking and analyzing followed by fifteen minutes of gazing at clouds. For very complex problems or following intense conscious work periods, you may even need to take a longer break. You can follow your intuition and also consider your schedule to decide what works best. Experiment with it and find your own sweet spot. We already do some of these steps intuitively, but if we bring more awareness into the process, we can fine-tune and get better at it over time with practice.

Key Takeaways

- Your intuition is a unique and powerful guide, and as you have explored and adapted the techniques in this book, I hope you've uncovered more ways to deepen your connection with this inner wisdom, enriching your life with insights, wonder, and clarity.
- You can also tap into your intuition with a playful journey—meeting a wise friend, or your younger or older self, or discovering notes from your future self. This imaginative exercise can unlock surprising insights, offering clarity and wisdom in a fun and personal way.
- By using familiar settings and objects we love, such as a train ride or a visit to an animal rescue, we can access our deeper emotional landscapes, allowing us to explore past experiences or current feelings.
- Intuition offers subtle yet powerful guidance for navigating future situations, helping you uncover perspectives that lead to more confident and aligned decisions.
- Our intuition, when paired with conscious analysis, can provide valuable insights into the timeline and potential obstacles of our goals, helping us navigate potential challenges and opportunities on the path.
- Automatic writing, a practice where you let your intuition guide the pen without conscious control, can unlock deep emotions and connect you with your inner wisdom, offering valuable insights when done regularly.
- By stepping back and observing a situation from a distance (such as putting it on a stage or in a dark room), you can gain intuitive clarity that helps you

navigate your emotions and relationships with greater understanding.

- When you focus your attention on one element and intentionally push distractions into the background, it becomes easier to quiet your mind, sharpen your focus, and connect more deeply with your intuition.
- Immersing yourself in a vivid, sensory-rich visualization of a place that sparks your creativity can unlock powerful intuitive insights, guiding you toward potential next steps.
- When a word pops into your mind, playfully explore it through visualization or song, allowing your intuition to reveal deeper meanings and guide you to new insights.
- By alternating periods of focused thinking with relaxation and creative breaks, you can tap into the power of both fast and slow intuition, allowing fresh ideas and insights to emerge naturally.

Reflections

- How has your relationship with your intuition evolved throughout this book? What insights have you gained about how it communicates with you?
- In what areas of your life have you already started to tap into your intuition? How has that shaped your experiences or decisions?
- Reflecting on the exercises from earlier chapters, as well as this one, what practices or techniques have felt most aligned with you? What makes them resonate with

your unique way of connecting to your inner wisdom?

- What new ways or methods can you experiment with to deepen your connection to your intuition? How might you adapt the ideas from this chapter to suit your lifestyle and needs?

- Consider a recent situation where your intuition guided you. How did you recognize its voice, and what outcome did it lead to?

- Looking ahead, how do you plan to integrate your intuition more fully into your daily life—wedding it with the input from your logical, problem-solving mind? What steps can you take to make this connection a regular and playful part of your routine?

Closing Words

The tips, tools, and techniques in this book are always here to inspire you to find your own ways to bring your intuition down to earth as well as provide guidance on your journey, and serve as reminders to connect with your inner wisdom in fun and practical ways. Please remember that intuition is a deeply personal ability, as much as it is universal. It works differently for every single one of us, in accordance with our unique gifts, talents, and life experiences—and it can even work differently for the same person during different life phases. No one knows you as well as you do, so I encourage you to come up with your own ways of priming and tapping into your intuition. I hope everything you've learned so far feels meaningful and relevant to your life. And may you always remember to blend your inner wisdom with logical analysis, research, and expert opinions, creating a harmonious balance that supports you on your journey.

SOURCES

Adinolfi, P, (2021). "A journey around decision-making: Searching for the 'big picture' across disciplines," *European Management Journal, Elsevier*, vol. 39(1), 9–21, ideas.repec.org/a/eee/eurman/v39y2021i1p9-21.html

Ambady, N., & Rosenthal, R. (1993). "Half a minute: Predicting teacher evaluations from thin slices of nonverbal behavior and physical attractiveness." *Journal of Personality and Social Psychology*, 64(3), 431–441, doi.org/10.1037/0022-3514.64.3.431

Bechara, A., Damasio, A. R., Damasio, H., & Anderson, S. W. (1994). "Insensitivity to future consequences following damage to human prefrontal cortex." *Cognition*, 50(1-3), 7–15, doi.org/10.1016/0010-0277(94)90018-3

Bolte, A., & Goschke, T. (2005). "On the speed of intuition: Intuitive judgments of semantic coherence under different response deadlines." *Memory & Cognition*, 33(7), 1248–1255, doi.org/10.3758/BF03193226

Bolte, A., Goschke, T., & Kuhl, J. (2003). "Emotion and intuition: Effects of positive and negative mood on implicit judgments of semantic coherence." *Psychological Science*, 14(5), 416–421, doi.org/10.1111/1467-9280.01456

Bowers, K. S., Regehr, G., Balthazard, C., & Parker, K. (1990). "Intuition in the context of discovery." *Cognitive Psychology*, 22(1), 72–110, doi.org/10.1016/0010-0285(90)90004-N

Ceci, S. J., & Bronfenbrenner, U. (1985). "Don't forget to take the cupcakes out of the oven: Prospective memory, strategic time-monitoring, and context." *Child Development*, 56(1), 152–164, doi.org/10.2307/1130182

Chamine, S. (2012). *Positive Intelligence: Why Only 20% of Teams and Individuals Achieve Their True Potential and How You Can Achieve Yours.* Greenleaf Book Group Press.

Cirillo, Francesco. *The Pomodoro Technique: The Acclaimed Time-Management System That Has Transformed How We Work.* Crown Publishing Group, 2018.

Claxton, G. (1999). *Hare Brain, Tortoise Mind: How Intelligence Increases When You Think Less.* London: Fourth Estate.

Cohen, M., Prather, A., Town, P., & Hynd, G. (1990). "Neurodevelopmental differences in emotional prosody in normal children and children with left and right temporal lobe epilepsy." *Brain and Language,* 38(1), 122–134, doi.org/10.1016/0093-934x(90)90105-p

Csikszentmihalyi, M. (1990). *Flow: The Psychology of Optimal Experience,* Harper Perennial Modern Classics; 1st edition.

Damásio, A. R. (1994). *Descartes' Error: Emotion, Reason, and the Human Brain.* New York: G.P. Putnam.

Dane, E., & Pratt, M. G. (2007). "Exploring intuition and its role in managerial decision making." *Academy of Management Review,* 32(1), 33–54, doi.org/10.2307/20159279

Dijksterhuis, A., & Nordgren, L. F. (2006). "A theory of unconscious thought." *Perspectives on Psychological Science,* 1(2), 95–109, doi.org/10.1111/j.1745-6916.2006.00007.x

Fogg, B.J. (2020). *Tiny Habits: The Small Changes That Change Everything.* New York: Houghton Mifflin Harcourt.

Gilhooly, K. J. (2016). "Incubation and intuition in creative problem solving." *Frontiers in Psychology,* 7, Article 1076, www.frontiersin.org/journals/psychology/articles/10.3389/fpsyg.2016.01076/full

HeartMath.org Intuition Research, www.heartmath.org/research/research-library/

Julmi, C. (2019). "When rational decision-making becomes irrational: A critical assessment and re-conceptualization of intuition effectiveness." *Business Research*, 12(1), 291–314, doi.org/10.1007/s40685-019-0096-4

Kahneman, D. (2011). *Thinking, Fast and Slow*. New York: Farrar, Straus and Giroux.

Kimsey-House, H., Kimsey-House, K., Sandahl, P., and Whitworth, L. (2018). *Co-Active Coaching: The Proven Framework for Transformative Conversations at Work and in Life* (4th ed.). London: Nicholas Brealey Publishing.

Klein, G. (1999). *Sources of Power: How People Make Decisions*. Cambridge, MA: MIT Press.

Lakoff, G., & Johnson, M. *Metaphors We Live By*. Chicago: University of Chicago Press, 1980.

Lewicki, P., Czyzewska, M., & Hoffman, H. (1987). "Unconscious acquisition of complex procedural knowledge." *Journal of Experimental Psychology: Learning, Memory, and Cognition*, 13(4), 523–530, doi.org/10.1037/0278-7393.13.4.523

Lieberman, M. D. (2000). "Intuition: A social cognitive neuroscience approach." *Psychological Bulletin*, 126(1), 109–137, doi.org/10.1037/0033-2909.126.1.109

Lufityanto, G., Donkin, C., & Pearson, J. (2016). "Measuring intuition: Nonconscious emotional information boosts decision accuracy and confidence." *Psychological Science*, 27(5), 622–634, doi.org/10.1177/0956797616629403

Pavlov, I. P. (1927). "Conditioned reflexes: An investigation of the physiological activity of the cerebral cortex." Oxford University Press, www.psychologywizard.net/uploads/2/6/6/4/26640833/pavlov_lecture_18.pdf

Pearson, J. (2024). *The Intuition Toolkit: The New Science of Knowing What without Knowing Why.* Simon & Schuster Australia.

Reber, A. S. (1967). "Implicit learning of artificial grammars." *Journal of Verbal Learning and Verbal Behavior,* 6(6), 855–863, doi.org/10.1016/S0022-5371(67)80149-X

Remmers, C., & Michalak, J. (2016). "Losing your gut feelings. Intuition in depression." *Frontiers in Psychology,* 7, Article 1291, www.ncbi.nlm.nih.gov/pmc/articles/PMC4993771/

Stoddard, J. A., & Afari, N. (2014). *The Big Book of ACT Metaphors: A Practitioner's Guide to Experiential Exercises and Metaphors in Acceptance and Commitment Therapy.* Oakland, CA: New Harbinger Publications.

Zander, T., Öllinger, M., & Volz, K. G. (2016). "Intuition and insight: Two processes that build on each other or fundamentally differ?" *Frontiers in Psychology,* 7, Article 1395, doi.org/10.3389/fpsyg.2016.01395

ACKNOWLEDGMENTS

There are so many people I want to thank here. My multitalented editor Nirmala Nataraj infused this book with her light and magic. The wonderful team at KN Literary Arts held my hand and guided me along this journey every step of the way. Elisabeth Rinaldi went through my manuscript diligently and was a joy to work with. Jill Esplin and Sheryl Zajechowski made me feel comfortable with the whole process from the onset. Karen Sommerfeld proofread the final draft meticulously. Christina Thiele designed the beautiful cover and layout.

My scientist husband, Dominic Hughes, believed that intuition had a role in solving difficult problems and encouraged me to write this book. My dear mom, Su Danis, taught me to be brave enough to take on any challenge as long as my heart was in it. My brother Murat Demircubuk made sure I was taken care of when I got carried away with writing.

Nancy Ancowitz, Pawan Bareja, Senia Maymin, Sabrina Moyle, Meir Schneider, and Zachary Shore generously took time from their busy writing and teaching schedules to review my book and share their wisdom and experience.

My chosen sisters and brothers Alev Akyol, Yasemin Ulusarac, Nurgul Balac, Aruna Bhamadipati, Inesssa Brovarnik, Lenka Beranova, Derya Cetiner, Jules De Jesus Fritz, Riza and Tanyeli Demirer, Zehra Donmez Turkoz, Ayse Evrensel, Dilber Duran Fanourgiakis, Lale Gunaydin, Hulya Gurer, Anja Hunsche, Vineet Kapur, Yasemin Khan, Dilhan Kellenberger, Hakan Koklu, Didem Kurt, Yesim Kustepeli, Stephanie Lee, Beth Mohr, Jamileh Musa, Susy Ortega,

Delynn Schor, Merve Sevinc, Elvan Tugsuz Guven, Aytac Yilmaz, and Aysegul Yonet sustained me with their love and friendship. Our walks and long chats over tea and lattes kept me going.

My coaching school sisters Sonya Orme and Lorraine Needham coached me beautifully to show me how much writing this book meant to me when I didn't even know where to begin.

My teacher Suze Allen filled my life with sparks of creative joy and made writing possible, fun, and essential.

My dear clients and students taught me how intuition worked so similarly and also so differently for each person and asked for this book.

All my friends and family who are not named here kept me company on my path all along. Thank you all for being you and being there for me.

ABOUT THE AUTHOR

Nil Demircubuk is an intuition facilitator and guide with more than three decades of experience. She is also a certified professional coach. She empowers her clients and students to get in touch with their own intuition and combine it with their intellect to make better decisions, improve their relationships and performance, and live more fulfilled lives.

Nil has reinvented herself multiple times as a result of significant health and other challenges. This ignited her passion to guide others in their journey through transformation. She studied engineering, obtained a PhD in economics, taught economics, ran the data group in a financial technology firm as a senior director, and led human-rights awareness programs in nonprofit organizations prior to shifting her focus to intuition facilitation and her coaching career.

Nil loves activities that put her in the flow state and prime her intuition, such as learning and practicing musical instruments and taking quiet walks in nature. She lives in California with her husband, and they travel to Europe regularly to visit family and friends.

If you'd like to study with Nil or book an intuitive session with her, you can reach her at nildemircubuk.com.